THE CROMFORD & HIGH PEAK RAILWAY

By
A. Rimmer

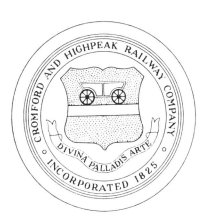

THE OAKWOOD PRESS

© The Oakwood Press 1985

ISBN 0 85361 319 2

Printed and bound by
S&S Press, Abingdon, Oxon

First printed November 1956
Reprinted January 1960
    „   November 1962
    „   October 1967
    „   October 1970
    „   October 1974
    „   May 1978
New Edition 1985

Published by
The OAKWOOD PRESS
P.O. Box 122, Headington, Oxford

An Enthusiasts Special train climbing Hopton Incline, headed by two North London Railway 0–6–0T locomotives.
LGRP, Courtesy David and Charles

Hard at work, nearing the top of the Hopton Incline is an ex-North London Railway 0–6–0T No. 58856. *Courtesy of the Derbyshire Advertiser*

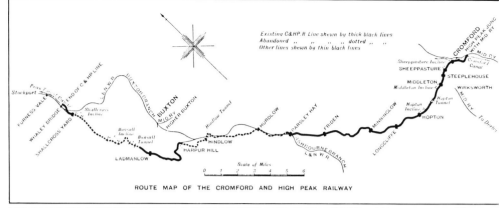

ROUTE MAP OF THE CROMFORD AND HIGH PEAK RAILWAY

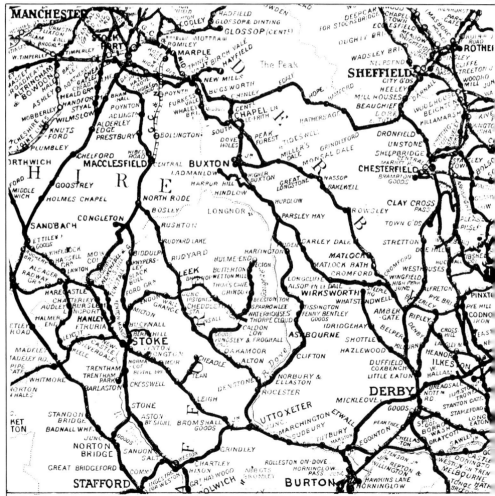

RCH map of 1920 showing the Cromford and High Peak Railway and railways in the associated area.

Contents

LNWR 2–4–0T sporting its new BR number, 58092, near Black Rocks.
LGRP, Courtesy David and Charles

CROMFORD AND HIGH PEAK RAILWAY.

NOTICE IS HEREBY GIVEN,

THAT the first General Meeting of the Company of Proprietors of the Cromford and High Peak Railway, will, in pursuance of an Act of Parliament made and passed in the sixth year of the reign of his present Majesty King George the Fourth, entitled " An Act for making and maintaining a Railway or Tramroad from the Cromford Canal, at or near to Cromford, in the parish of Wirksworth, in the county of Derby, to the Peak Forest Canal, at or near to Whaley, (otherwise Yardsley cum Whaley,) in the county palatine of Chester," be held at the house of Mrs. Cummings, the Old Bath, Matlock, in the county of Derby, on Thursday, the twenty-sixth day of May instant, at Eleven o'clock in the Forenoon, for the purpose of proceeding in the execution of the said Act.— Dated this third day of May, 1825.

CROMFORD AND HIGH PEAK RAILWAY.
TO CONTRACTORS.

THE COMMITTEE of MANAGEMENT of the CROMFORD and HIGH PEAK RAILWAY, are prepared to receive TENDERS for the execution of a BRANCH LINE from the Manchester, Buxton, Matlock, and Midlands Junction Railway, to the terminus of the Comford and High Peak Railway, near Cromford, a distance of 58 Chains.

The Committee will meet at the GREYHOUND INN, Cromford, on SATARDAY, the 16th instant, at Eleven o'clock in the Forenoon, to LET the WORK, when Parties Tendering must attend.

By order, FRANCIS BARTON, Agent.
Railway Office, Cromford, 4th Oct., 1852.

Top: A notice which appeared in the *Derby Reporter* 5 May 1825 advertising a meeting of proprietors of the C & HPR Co. at which the Act of Parliament was to be discussed.

Bottom: This advertisement appeared in the *Derby Mercury* on 6 October 1852 and dealt with the extension from Cromford Wharf to the MBM & MJR at the point which later became High Peak Junction.

The Cromford & High Peak Railway
Chapter 1
Early History

"The skyscraping High Peak Railway with its corkscrew curves that seem to have been laid out by a mad Archimedes endeavouring to square the circle." Thus did one nineteenth-century writer, dealing with scenery in the Derbyshire Peak District, endeavour to describe the Cromford & High Peak Railway. And, indeed, anyone who visited the line as it wound its way over the wild moors and round the limestone crags of northern Derbyshire may be moved to echo these words.

It was in May 1825, soon after the opening of the Stockton and Darlington Railway, that the first Act of Parliament was passed "for making and maintaining a Railway or Tram Road, from the Cromford Canal, at or near to Cromford, in the parish of Wirksworth, in the County of Derby, to the Peak Forest Canal at or near to Whaley in the County Palatine of Chester". Earlier, it had been proposed that this should be effected by means of a canal, but, owing to the difficulty of ensuring an adequate water supply on the moors, this scheme was dropped, and the alternative, a railway, was put forward. The railway was built on a similar alignment to that which would have been followed if the canal had been constructed. This involved steep inclined planes, worked by stationary engines and continuous chains, taking the place of what would have been flights of locks. Cromford is 277 ft above sea level, and the summit of the line at Ladmanlow was 1,264 ft above sea level (sometimes quoted as 1,266 ft); from Ladmanlow the line drops in 8 miles to 517 ft above datum at Whaley Bridge: this gives some idea of the severe task which faced the engineer, Josias Jessop.

In the first of the Acts, which was dated 2 May 1825, the Cromford & High Peak Railway was envisaged as "a Railway or Tramroad for passage of waggons and other carriages, to be propelled thereon by Stationary or Locomotive Steam Engines or other sufficient power".

The object of constructing the railway was because it "will open up a more easy and commodious communication between the agricultural and mineral counties of Derby, Nottingham and Leicester, and other eastern and southern counties, and the great manufacturing towns of Stockport and Manchester, and other large and populous districts and will otherwise be of great public utility by facilitating the conveyance of coal, iron, lime, corn,

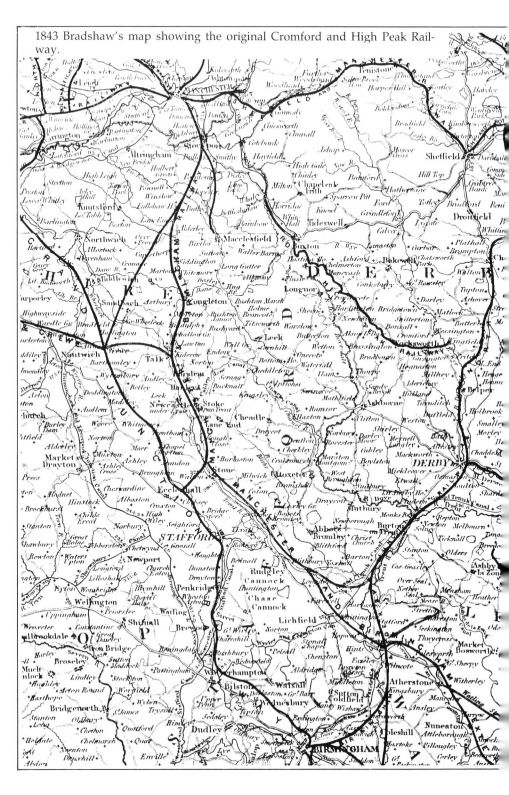

1843 Bradshaw's map showing the original Cromford and High Peak Railway.

minerals and other commodities from the several beforementioned counties to the said towns of Stockport and Manchester and other extensive and populous districts, and also the conveyance of merchandise and other commodities from such towns and districts to and into the interior of the said counties".

A clause was inserted to the effect that "the furnace of every Stationary Steam engine . . . to be constructed upon the principle of consuming its own smoke".

A capital of £164,400 was to be raised by the company in £100 shares, together with £32,880 in loans. Also included in the Act was a provision that no four-wheeled wagon should carry more than six tons, including tare, and that no six-wheeled wagon should carry more than nine tons including tare. Clause CXXII stated that, if the railway was not completed within seven years, then the powers for its construction would cease.

The total length of the line was 33 miles, and it was opened in two sections. The first section, from Cromford Wharf to Hurdlow, a distance of 15½ miles, came into use on 29 May 1830. Just over a year later, on 6 July 1831, the remaining 17½ miles to Whaley Bridge were opened "to the public for general trade". A notice to the effect that this would take place appeared in the *Stockport Advertiser* dated Friday, 1 July 1831.

A description of the first portion of the line was given in the *Derby Mercury* dated Wednesday, 2 June 1830:

On Saturday last the south eastern end of the Cromford & High Peak Railway was put into operation for the conveyance of goods to the extent of about 15 miles, which will supply with coal the districts surrounding Wirksworth, Brassington, Bradbourne, Parwich, Winster, Youlgreave, Moneyash, Hartington, Longnor, etc., the inhabitants of which places have for long felt the inconvenience and expense of bringing the coal from a distance and carting up steep hills where the quantity taken by a horse must necessarily be small.

The railway was opened in a private manner by drawing about 100 tons of coal up four of the inclined planes, the greatest part of which was for the neighbourhood of Hartington, where, and in the adjacent places, the commencement of the coal trade on the railway has been anxiously looked for.

The four inclined planes now finished [these would be Cromford, Sheep Pasture, Middleton, and Hopton] attain an elevation of 810 ft above the canal, and from their summit, the railway is level for 12 miles. The remaining part of the line is in a state of forwardness and will ere long be completed. Up one of the planes, rising more than 250 ft, upwards of 90 tons of coal was drawn in one hour and twenty-five minutes.

Much has been said respecting the danger attending inclined planes, but on the Cromford and High Peak that has been obviated by a very simple apparatus attached to the wagons, denominated a 'Preventor', which will in all cases ensure safety whether ascending or descending. When we consider that a horse

Particulars of Gradients.

Miles.		Rising or Falling.	Gradient.	Between what Stations.		Locomotive or Stationary Engine.
From	To			From	To	
0	$1\frac{1}{8}$	Rising	1 in 120	High Peak Junction ...	Bottom of Sheep Pasture	Locomotive.
$1\frac{1}{8}$	$1\frac{7}{8}$	Rising	1 in $8\frac{1}{2}$	Sheep-pasture Incline	......	Stationary.
$1\frac{7}{8}$	$3\frac{1}{4}$	Level	...	Steeplehouse	Middle Peak Yard ...	Locomotive.
$3\frac{1}{4}$	$3\frac{7}{8}$	Rising	1 in $8\frac{1}{2}$	Middleton Incline ...	.. ...	Stationary.
$3\frac{7}{8}$	$5\frac{1}{8}$	Falling	1 in 1056	Middleton	Hopton	
$5\frac{1}{8}$	$5\frac{1}{4}$	Rising	1 in 14	Hopton Incline	......	
$5\frac{1}{4}$	7	Falling	1 in 792	Hopton	Longcliffe	
7	$8\frac{7}{8}$	Level	...	Longcliffe	Minninglow	
$8\frac{7}{8}$	$9\frac{3}{4}$	Falling	1 in 792	Longcliffe	Minninglow and Friden	
$9\frac{3}{4}$	$10\frac{3}{4}$	Rising	1 in 792	Minninglow	Friden	Locomotive.
$10\frac{3}{4}$	15	Rising	1 in 757	Minninglow	Parsley Hay	
15	$17\frac{1}{2}$	Level	...	Parsley Hay	Hurdlow	
$17\frac{1}{2}$	$19\frac{1}{2}$	Rising	1 in 60	Hurdlow	......	
$19\frac{1}{2}$	29	Level	...	Hurdlow	Bunsall	
29	$29\frac{3}{4}$	Falling	1 in 792	Hurdlow	Bunsall	
$29\frac{3}{4}$	$30\frac{3}{8}$	Falling	1 in $7\frac{1}{2}$	Bunsall Incline	......	Stationary.
$30\frac{3}{8}$	33	Level	...	Bunsall	Shallcross	Locomotive.
33	$33\frac{1}{2}$	Falling	1 in $10\frac{1}{2}$	Shallcross Incline ...	......	Stationary.
$33\frac{1}{2}$	$33\frac{5}{8}$	Level	...	Shallcross Yard	......	...
$33\frac{5}{8}$	$33\frac{3}{4}$	Falling	1 in $18\frac{1}{2}$	Whaley Bridge	......	Windlass.

Manchester,
April, 1891.

G. E. Mawby,
District Superintendent.

A gradient post between the upper and lower sections on the Sheep Pasture Incline.
LGRP, Courtesy David and Charles

102.—CROMFORD AND HIGH PEAK.

(LEASED IN PERPETUITY TO THE LONDON AND NORTH WESTERN.)

This old-established canal and tramway (6th Geo. IV., cap. 30) was re-incorporated by Act 18 and 19 Vic., cap. 75 (26th June, 1855). The undertaking consists of a railway from Peak Forest Canal to the Cromford Canal, and to a junction with the Manchester Buxton Matlock and Midlands Junction. The Cromford subscribes 3,750l. to the Stockport Disley and Whaley Bridge.

By 21 and 22 Vic., cap. 61 (28th June, 1858), the company was authorised to issue additional capital to the extent of 60,000l. at 6 per cent., on an equality with existing preference shares, and by borrowing to the extent of one-third of additional share capital.

By 25 and 26 Vic., cap. 66 (30th June, 1862), a lease to the London and North Western was authorised, and the capital re-arranged. This lease took effect on 25th March, 1861, at a rent of 3,500l. for the first year, and 4,000l. subsequently.

CAPITAL.—The expenditure on this account extends to 260,841l., which has been met as follows:—

Shares and stock	£167,700	
Loans	78,825	
Debenture stock	100	
Sundries, materials Sold, &c.	14,216	£260,841

The meetings may be held in Derby twice a-year, or at such times and places as the directors appoint. Quorum of shareholders, 5 ; qualification, 10,000l.

No. of Directors—10 ; minimum, 5 ; quorum, 3. *Qualification, 500l.*

DIRECTORS:

Chairman—FRANCIS WRIGHT, Esq., of Osmaston Manor, near Derby.

Robert Broom, Esq., Burbage, near Buxton.
Philip Hubbersty, Esq., Wirksworth.
William Jessop, Esq., Butterley Hall, near Alfreton.

John Wright. Esq., Osmaston Manor, near Derby.
James Charles Arkwright, Esq., Cromford.

OFFICERS.— Sec., Edward Lacey, Burbage, near Buxton ; Auditors, Nathaniel Wheatcroft, Jun., Cromford, and George Staley, Butterley.

Office—Burbage, Buxton.

Extract from Bradshaw's Railway Manual of 1870 concerning the Cromford and High Peak Railway.

LNWR 2–4–0T with train of wagons including two water tenders immediately behind the engine, in LMS days.   *LGRP, Courtesy David and Charles*

will on a level railway draw more than 10 tons of coal, while on a common road also level, he cannot draw more than one, the expense of carriage (which in Derbyshire higher parts forms more than 50 per cent of the cost to the consumer) must be diminished, and by the use of steam engines in drawing the wagons up the hills much expense is saved, as it is well known that animal power cannot compete with steam.

Apart from the inclined planes, operated by stationary engines, the rest of the line relied on horses for motive power. The traffic, which was minerals and goods only, took about two days to travel from one end of the line to the other. There still exists a relic of the horse working, in the form of stable doors built into the ground-floor walls of the stationmaster's house at Longcliffe. Another link with the early days is the winding engine at Middleton Top, the sole survivor of those originally installed, which was in use for winding until 1963, and for pumping thereafter until 1967. It has since been restored, and can be run on compressed air. Reference will be made to this engine later.

Steam power began to replace the horses in 1833, when the first locomotive was delivered. It took thirty years, however, before horse traction was entirely replaced by locomotives, and even then the noble animal found a niche for himself, operating the capstan on the Whaley Bridge Incline, until this was taken out of use on 9 April 1952.

The next Act affecting the line was passed in 1843. This dealt mainly with the financial position of the company and was "to enable the Cromford and High Peak Railway Co. to grant mortgages for part of the floating debts". It appears that when the railway was being built, the company "contracted debts for the supply of rails, stationary steam engines and other matters essential to the completion of the railway, which debts still remained owing". These debts had been run up "in and about the year 1830", and the total sum in debts and unpaid interest on 30 September 1842 amounted to £46,915. The company had found that the revenue from traffic had only been enough to cover the cost of working and maintaining the railway, so that they could not meet the interest charges, nor were they in a position to declare a dividend on their shares. This had resulted in a slump in the price of shares, and it was not possible to raise funds to meet the outstanding debts by a further subscription.

The Cromford & High Peak Railway did not remain in splendid isolation for very long. Physical connection was made with the Manchester, Buxton, Matlock & Midlands Junction Railway at High Peak Junction, about three-quarters of a mile from Cromford

An Allan "Crewe Goods" 2–4–0 locomotive at Hurdlow Top. The train includes the "fly" van in which passengers were carried, and in fact a lady awaits to board!
LGRP, Courtesy David and Charles

Middleton Top. This photograph shows well the winding house buildings, signal and cabin and catch points on both tracks. *LGRP, Courtesy David and Charles*

Wharf; this was brought into use on 21 February 1853. At the opposite end, an extension of a quarter of a mile giving access to the Stockport, Disley & Whaley Bridge Railway was opened on 17 August 1857. The Whaley Bridge spur was authorised by an Act of 1855, which also empowered the railway to make an improvement by "deviation of the line and levels, and an enlargement of the existing railway in the township of Hartington Upper Quarter, in the parish of Hartington, such deviation or enlargement to commence at or near the point in such township, where the new road from Macclesfield to Buxton crosses under the railway and terminates at or near the point where the old road from Macclesfield to Buxton crosses over the railway". Other alterations further south resulted in the abandonment of the 1 in 16 Hurdlow Incline, with a deviation line on a gradient of 1 in 60 making it possible for locomotives to work right through from the top of the Hopton Incline to the top of the Bunsall Incline .

The same Act also dealt with the company's finances. The fact that mortgages had been granted in respect of £22,890 appears in the preamble. Further reference was made to the financial state of the company, which was not particularly healthy. No dividend had been paid, and debts and interest charges still remained undischarged.

By the same Act also the company was given power to inaugurate a passenger service. This was done, and passengers were carried by certain trains, until, towards the end of the 1870s, an unfortunate person was killed as the result of an accident, and the company discontinued the service soon afterwards.

There had been a passenger service prior to this, provided by Messrs G. Wheatcroft under contract, and which had operated from May 1833. The same firm also operated a coach service between Whaley Bridge and Manchester in connection with the rail facility from Cromford, to enable passengers to go forward from the northern railhead.

In 1856 the chains which had been in use on the inclines since the railway was opened were replaced by hemp ropes on most of the inclines, and these in turn were superseded by steel wire ropes in 1861 and onwards. The Whaley Bridge Incline, however, continued to use chains until it was closed in 1952, and Hopton Incline was equipped in the same way until 1877, after which it was operated by locomotives.

The alterations carried out after the passing of the 1855 Act resulted in such an increase in traffic that in 1858 the company sought powers to improve the whole of the line. This, of course,

These two plates show Cromford Canal wharf and transit sheds. *Author's Collection*

required more funds, and the Act authorised the company to raise additional capital not exceeding £60,000 by the issue of 6 per cent preference shares of face value of £20, "at such times and in such manner as the directors from time to time determine".

In 1862 the Cromford & High Peak Railway (Lease) Act passed through Parliament. This Act leased the C&HP Railway to the London & North Western Railway for a period of nine hundred and ninety-nine years. Although this lease was not authorised until 30 June 1862, it was effective from 25 March of the previous year. Twenty-six years later, on 19 July 1887, the London & North Western Railway Act gave powers to the L&NWR and the Cromford & High Peak Railway to amalgamate, effective from 1 July 1887.

This acquisition paved the way for a thorough refashioning of the northern end of the C&HP, as part of a new through route from the south to Buxton. The LNWR was given power by an Act of 4 August 1890 to abandon the Cromford & High Peak Railway north of Ladmanlow, with the exception of a short stretch at Whaley Bridge. Authority was also given for the construction of a new line from Hindlow to Buxton, for re-alignment of the existing C&HP Railway between Parsley Hay and Ladmanlow, and for the building of a new line from Parsley Hay to Ashbourne. These works were completed in stages. The Hindlow to Ladmanlow re-alignment and the new line from Hindlow to Buxton was ready for use by 27 June 1892; two days previously the Ladmanlow--Shallcross section had been abandoned, and by 1894 the rails had been taken up. On 1 June 1894 the Hindlow–Parsley Hay re-alignment and doubling was ready for use, and the final stage, the line from Parsley Hay to Ashbourne, was opened on 4 August 1899.

The abandonment of such a considerable length of line in the 1890s may, at first sight, seem to call for explanation. With the opening of the Hindlow to Buxton section, an alternative route existed to Whaley Bridge, as the Stockport, Disley & Whaley Bridge Railway had been extended to Buxton by 15 June 1864, and had become part of the London & North Western system two years later. This alternative route had the decisive advantage, from the operating view-point, that it cut out the descent of the Bunsall and Shallcross Inclines, with their inevitable delays.

Other Acts of Parliament affected the Cromford & High Peak Railway indirectly. At the "grouping" of 1923 it became part of the London, Midland & Scottish Railway system, and then, on 1 January 1948, part of the all-embracing British Railways. Despite all this, however, it never lost its identity, and until closure, and beyond, it was referred to by enthusiasts and railwaymen alike as "the High Peak Railway".

Ladmanlow, showing the signal controlling the Grinn Branch, private siding of the Clay Cross Co. (*see pages 60 and 61*).
LGRP, Courtesy David and Charles

Chapter 2
The Route

For the benefit of the visitor to the area, and to enable the reader to visualise what it was like, this chapter describes the line from High Peak Junction towards Whaley Bridge, as it was in the 1950s when the book was first published, and deals with the salient features to be seen along the line at that time.

Leaving High Peak Junction (between Whatstandwell and Cromford stations on the Midland line), the single track climbs through dense woods to Cromford Goods a mile away. Approaching the goods yard the line is crossed by an ungated level crossing, control of which is by means of a crude semaphore signal. Simply a red-painted rectangular iron plate mounted on a vertical rod, it can be turned by hand through 90 degrees, so that it can either present the face of the plate to the railway line, permitting road traffic to use the crossing, or be edge-on to the approaching trains, indicating "All Clear" to the driver.

The Cromford Canal, now disused, is alongside the yard, and there is a large transit shed, with an awning projecting over the water, under which the barges were moored. Other buildings include the old workshops where the early locomotives were constructed and serviced, and where today the yard shunting engine spends its resting hours and repairs to the travelling water tanks are effected.

Cromford Goods Yard is at the bottom of Sheep Pasture Incline, the first of the inclined planes which are the most interesting feature of the Cromford & High Peak Railway. When the line was completed, there were nine of these planes, although some writers have stated that there were only eight. The discrepancy appears to have arisen from the fact that the Bunsall Incline between Ladmanlow and the Goyt Valley was, when the line was opened, two separate inclines, which were combined into one in 1857, having previously been called Bunsall Upper and Bunsall Lower. In the same year, two other inclines, namely Sheep Pasture and Cromford, were combined to form the present Sheep Pasture Incline, on which working as one incline began on 16 October 1857. The present incline rises at 1 in 9, and then 1 in 8, for a distance of 1,320 yards. Haulage is by means of a continuous wire rope which is 2,880 yards long. At the bottom the rope runs underground and is passed round a large pulley, situated in a pit built beneath the running tracks. At the top, the rope once again goes underground, into the winding engine house which is at the left-hand side of the line, as the wagons approach the summit. Inside the engine house

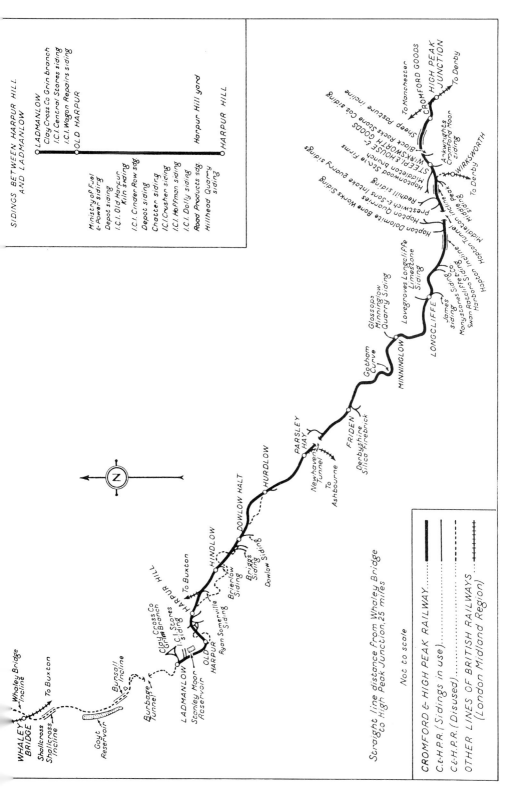

SIDINGS BETWEEN HARPUR HILL
AND LADMANLOW

LADMANLOW
Clay Cross Co Grin branch
I.C.I. Central Stores siding
I.C.I. Wagon Repairs siding
OLD HARPUR

Ministry of Fuel & Power siding
Depot siding
I.C.I. Old Harpur Kiln siding
I.C.I. Cinder Row sdg
Depot siding
Chatter siding
I.C.I. Crusher siding
I.C.I. Hoffman siding
I.C.I. Dolly siding
Road Products sdg.
Hillhead Quarry siding
Harpur Hill yard

HARPUR HILL

N

WHALEY BRIDGE
Whaley Bridge Incline
To Buxton
Shallcross Shallcross Incline
Gayt. Reservoir
Burbage Tunnel
Bunsall Incline
Stanley Moon Reservoir
LADMANLOW
OLD HARPUR
HARPUR HILL
Clay Cross Co Grin branch
I.C.I. Stones siding
Ryan Somerville Siding
Brierlow Siding
Briggs Siding
To Buxton
HINDLOW
Dowlow Siding
DOWLOW HALT
HURDLOW
Newhaven Tunnel
To Ashbourne
PARSLEY HAY
FRIDEN
Derbyshire Silica Firebrick
Gotham Curve
MINNINGLOW
Glossops Minninglow Quarry Siding
Lovegroves Longcliffe Limestone Siding
LONGCLIFFE
James siding
Monystones Siding Co
Manystones Freestone siding
Swan Ratcliff Incline siding
Harboro Siding
Hopton Wood Stone Co
Hopton Dolomite Bone Works Siding
Hopton Quarries
Prestwich & Sons Intake Quarry sidings
Redhill siding
Hoptonwood Stone Co firms
Middleton branch
Middleton Tunnel
STEEPLE HOUSE & WIRKSWORTH GOODS
Block Rocks Stone Co's siding
Sheep pasture incline
Cromford Moor siding
Arkwrights
WIRKSWORTH
To Denby
To Manchester
CROMFORD GOODS
HIGH PEAK JUNCTION
To Denby

Straight line distance from Whaley Bridge
to High Peak Junction, 25 miles

Not to scale

CROMFORD & HIGH PEAK RAILWAY............
C & H.P.R. (Sidings in use)....................
C & H.P.R. (Disused).............................
OTHER LINES OF BRITISH RAILWAYS...........
(London Midland Region)

the rope passes round a large pulley, 14 ft 1 in. in diameter, after which it passes round the driving pulley, which is the same size and is vertically underneath the loose pulley. This method increases the arc of contact between the rope and the driving pulley and also avoids any reverse bends in the rope.

The winding engine at Sheep Pasture Top is a relatively modern twin-cylinder horizontal type, which drives the original flywheel and pulley through bevel gears. It was built in 1883, and its cylinders of 17 in. bore by 24 in. stroke are supplied with steam at 80 pounds per square inch from an old locomotive boiler, which is fired mainly with wood.

The wagons are attached in "runs" to the wire ropes by means of tapering chains, which are plaited round the rope and their ends secured by leather straps. The maximum permitted weight of a run is 38 tons, and the weight of the descending run is usually arranged to be slightly more than that of the corresponding one ascending. In this way, the engine is only necessary for controlling the speed of the run.

Signalling on the incline is primitive but effective. Although an ex-LNWR semaphore signal is situated at the top of the incline, it is no longer used, and a series of bells and pointers at the top and bottom of the slope are connected by wires. The pointer in the engine house at Sheep Pasture Top, had three positions, one being "B" for *Stand By*, "G" for *Go*, and "S" for *Stop*. The bells are arranged to ring when the pointer is moved.

Near the bottom of the incline, the two running tracks widen out and pass on each side of a large sleeper-lined pit, into which lead two spurs from catch points situated above the pit. This was constructed after an accident which occurred on 1 March 1888, when two wagons forming a descending run broke away soon after leaving the Top and ran freely down the full length of the incline. By the time they reached the bottom, they were moving very fast and failed to negotiate the curve into the goods yard at Cromford Wharf. Instead, they leapt across the Cromford Canal, cleared the two tracks of the Midland Railway, which at that point are some fifteen or twenty feet below the level of the canal, and finally came to rest in a field, completely wrecked. The wagons concerned formed the last run of the day, and were a brake van and a load of limestone which had come in on the second train from Hurdlow Top. Fortunately the guard and another railwayman who were riding in the van jumped clear when the breakaway occurred, so no one was hurt.

A graphic description of another breakaway has been given by

Two views of High Peak Junction. The top view is looking south, off the High Peak line. The Signalbox just behind the P.O. wagons is controlling the lines to Matlock and Manchester; this line runs to the left behind the hut. The lower view shows (*from left to right*) the down siding and High Peak line, the up and down main lines and the up loop on the extreme right. *LRGP, Courtesy David and Charles*

Cromford Wharf showing the transit shed beyond the crossing and protected by the banner signal, seen here in the "stop" position to rail traffic.

LGRP, Courtesy David and Charles

LMS 0–6–0T, No. 6428 shunting P.O. wagons at High Peak Junction sidings in May 1940.

H.C. Casserley

Looking down from the road bridge over the incline at Sheep Pasture Bottom.

Derbyshire Advertiser

Two views taken from Sheep Pasture Bottom Incline. the engineman's "bothy" is seen behind the signal with the workshops beyond. The watertank was fed from a spring in the hillside. The lower photograph shows well the crew hut at the bottom of the incline with workman and bike ascending. *Note*: The "workman" is in fact Sam Buckley who spent his whole railway working life on the C&HP as cleaner, fireman and driver. At the time of the photograph, he was a cleaner. *H.C. Casserley*

Another view of the catchpoints and pointsman's cabin on Sheep Pasture Incline. The incline "gong" and cable pulley system is clearly visible in this 1958 view.

Derbyshire Advertiser

A J94 class 0–6–0ST, No. 68012 standing at Sheep Pasture Bottom. The incline is round to the left.

Author's Collection

An old view of 1904 showing a Crewe Goods 2–4–0T ascending Sheep Pasture Incline on the winding rope. Note the catchpoints and gravel run away dragpit between the two running tracks.   *LGRP, Courtesy David and Charles*

A general view of Sheep Pasture Incline showing the descending run, passing catchpit and pointsman's cabin (just above the convergence of tracks).   *Derbyshire Advertiser*

LM&SR

CROMFORD ENGINE HOUSE

SHEEP PASTURE TOP

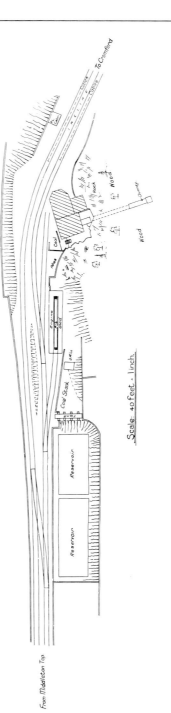

From Middleton Top

Scale: 40 feet = 1 inch.

Reservoir

Reservoir

Coal Stack

Office

Engine P.G. Office

Coal

Shed

Coal

Track

Wood

Wood

To Cromford

Sheep Pasture Top as seen from the middle of the incline looking towards the locomotive shed, engine house (distance) and the water reservoir on the right.

LGRP, Courtesy David and Charles

View of Catchpit Sheep Pasture Incline with a mobile water tank and wagon ascending.

Courtesy Derbyshire Advertiser

CROMFORD & HIGH PEAK LINE.

STEEPLEHOUSE.

Black Rocks Stone & Sand Co's Siding.

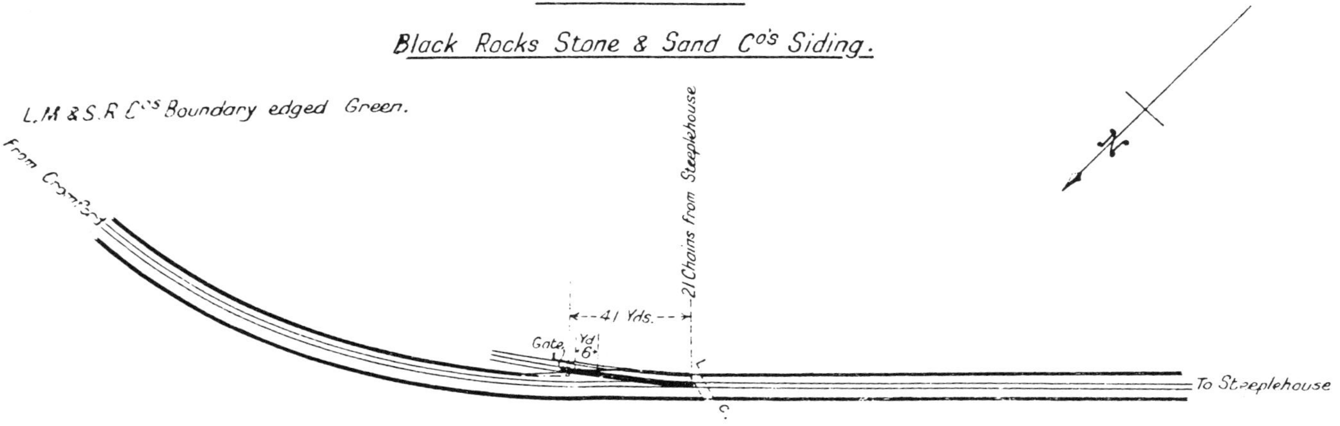

L.M. & S.R. Co's Boundary edged Green.

From Cromford

21 Chains from Steeplehouse

To Steeplehouse

Gate Yd
6'

41 Yds.

N

CROMFORD & HIGH PEAK LINE.

STEEPLEHOUSE.

Cromford Moor Siding.

Between 21½ & 21¾ M.P.s

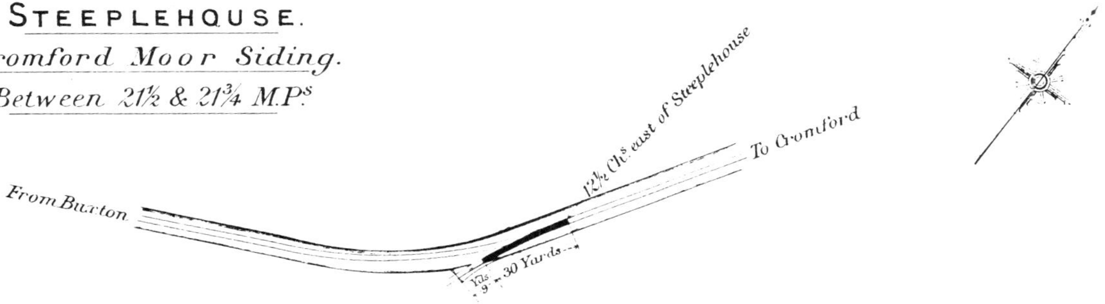

From Buxton

1¾ Ch. east of Steeplehouse

To Cromford

7½ Yds.
30 Yds.
9'

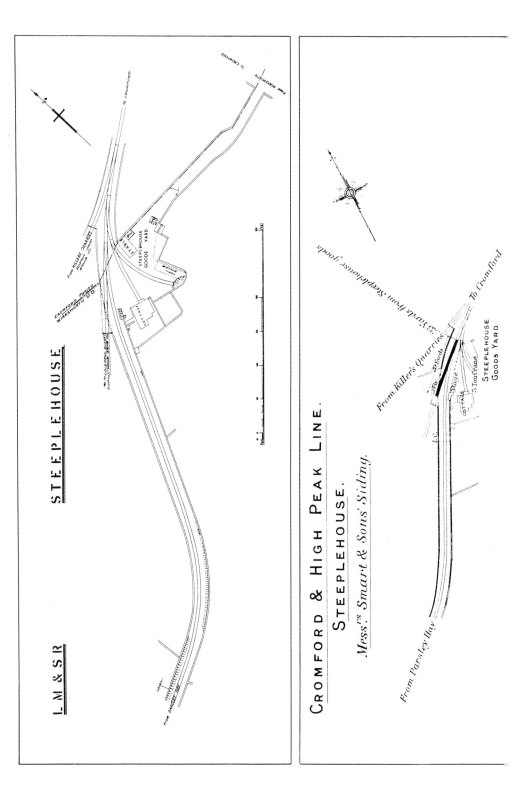

STEEPLEHOUSE

L M & S R

CROMFORD & HIGH PEAK LINE.
STEEPLEHOUSE.
Mess.rs Smart & Sons' Siding.

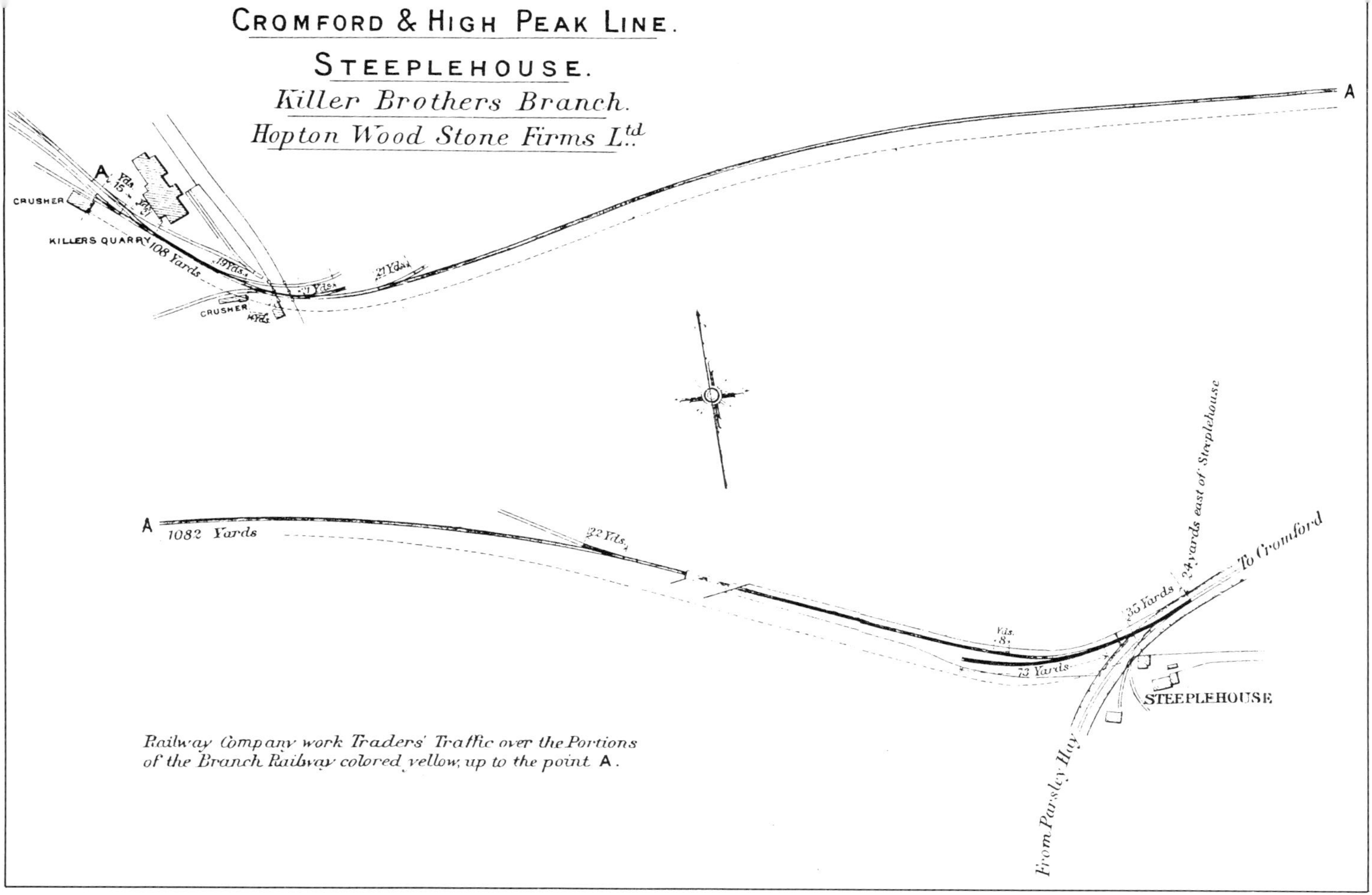

CROMFORD & HIGH PEAK LINE.

STEEPLEHOUSE.

Killer Brothers Branch.
Hopton Wood Stone Firms L.^{td}...

To Cromford

230yards east of Steeplehouse

8 sprbes, 240yards

STEEPLEHOUSE

From Parsley Hay

22 Yds.

57 Yards

Yds.
8.

22 Yds.

A   1082 Yards

CRUSHER

KILLERS QUARRY 108 Yards

CRUSHER

Yds.
15 · 22

CRUSHER

A

Railway Company work Traders' Traffic over the Portions
of the Branch Railway colored yellow, up to the point A.

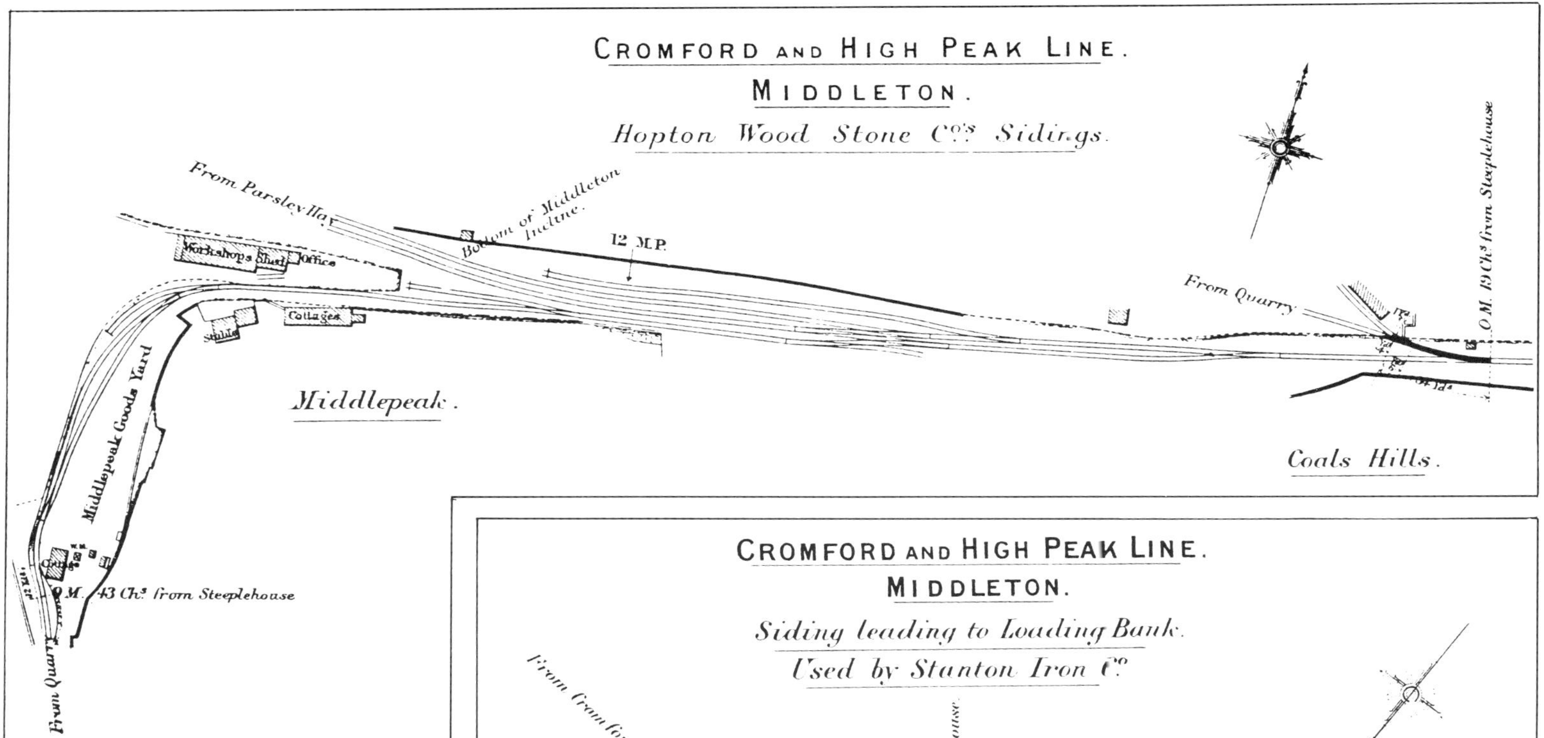

CROMFORD and HIGH PEAK LINE.

MIDDLETON.

Hopton Wood Stone C^{os} Sidings.

O.M. 19 Ch^s from Steeplehouse.

Coals Hills.

From Quarry.

12 M.P.

Tram of Middleton

From Parsley Hay

Middlepeak.

Workshops Shed Office

Coke Oven

Weigh

Middlepeak Goods Yard

43 Ch^s from Steeplehouse

From Quarry

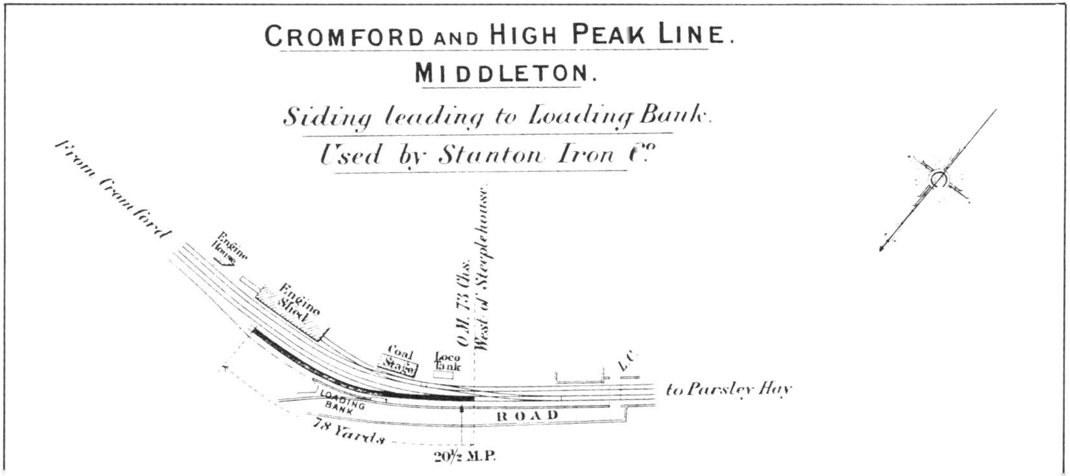

CROMFORD and HIGH PEAK LINE.

MIDDLETON.

Siding leading to loading Bank.
Used by Stanton Iron C^o.

to Parsley Hay

L.C.

ROAD

O.M. 75 Ch^s West of Steeplehouse

Loco Bank

Coal Wagon

20½ M.P.

78 Yards

LOADING BANK

Engine Shed.

Engine House

From Cromford

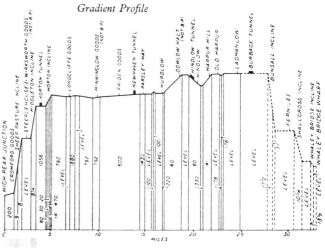

Gradient Profile

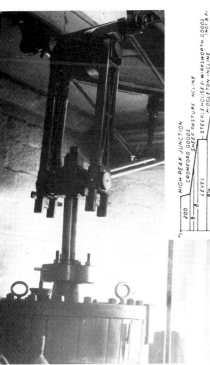

The winding engine at Middleton Incline in 1934.

H.C. Casserley

The same engine, showing (*from left to right*) flywheel, top winding pulley and main cylinders and valve chests.

Author's Collection

Middleton Top gradient post and catch point lever for "down" going traffic on the 1 in 8¼ fall.

LGRP, Courtesy David and Charles

View of locomotive shed, engine-man's cottage and, behind, Middleton engine house with No. 58860 on shed.

LGRP, Courtesy David and Charles

Mr A. Ranson Cowlishaw, who witnessed it.* This was after the catch pit was constructed, as reference is made to "the pointsman fleeing for dear life down the field in the direction of Cromford, whilst the trucks smashed to matchwood in the catch pit".

Some time after this, a wagon left the rope below the catch points, and this wagon also cleared the canal and, the reference says, "finished up intact in the field on the near side of the Midland Railway. It is fortunate it went no further, as an express from St. Pancras to Manchester was just due". Some doubt must be attached to this, as there is only a farm track, and not a field, between the canal and the Midland main line at this point, and it is likely that this wagon also cleared both the canal and the railway.

The provision of the catch pit meant that, whenever the incline was in use, a pointsman had to be on duty to pull the points for the down-coming wagons to prevent them running into the pit, as the points were normally set in that direction by springs. To enable the pointsman to judge the speed of the approaching wagons, gongs operated by wires and treadles which are depressed by the wheel flanges of the passing wagons are provided in a cabin by the points. From the time interval between the gongs sounding, the pointsman can judge if the wagons are under control or not; if so, he pulls the points accordingly.

A unique gradient post used to be situated on the Sheep Pasture Incline, which indicated a change of gradient from 1 in 8 to 1 in 9. The provision of this post, shown in the photograph on page 10, is interesting, but whether it served any useful purpose is a matter for conjecture.

The line between Sheep Pasture Top and Middleton Bottom is virtually level, and in fact, when it is compared with the inclined planes, the remainder of the Cromford & High Peak Railway line appears to have very little of interest to offer. This impression is borne out by the gradient diagram, which shows, apart from the planes, few pitches as steep as one might expect, considering the type of country which the line traverses. The engineer achieved this by following the contours of the land closely, cutting through the rock where necessary, and constructing suitable embankments where valleys or depressions had to be crossed. There are several of these on the section between Longcliffe Goods and Friden; the most impressive of these is one near Minninglow. The embankments are faced with limestone blocks, and although it cannot be said that they blend well into the landscape, yet they could never be classed as an eyesore. Someone once said that the Minninglow embankment viewed in the light of the setting sun on a summer's

* *Railway Magazine*, vol. 77 (July 1935), p. 62.

evening is a sight to be remembered.

Immediately after leaving Sheep Pasture Top, the line runs past the engine shed and a reservoir. With trees and bracken on both sides, and with one or two small cuttings *en route*, the massive outcrop known as Black Rocks is reached, the track appearing insignificant as it skirts the base. Swinging to the right across an embankment, and immediately after crossing the Cromford to Wirksworth road, we arrive at Steeplehouse and Wirksworth Goods. It was in the yard here that on 30 July 1955 engine No. 47000 made news by toppling down a 15 ft embankment into the garden of Station House, where it ended up wheels in the air.

Near the bottom of the Middleton Incline there can be seen on the left the earthworks which were constructed for an incline linking up with the Midland Railway station at Wirksworth. This scheme never reached fruition, although the winding engine house was partially constructed.

The small yard on the left is called Middle Peak Siding, and it must have been at this point, or nearby, that the proposed Ashbourn [*sic*] and Wirksworth railway would have linked up with the C&HPR. The author has a copy of the original scheme prepared by Thos. Woodhouse in 1827, and this provided two routes. One of these would have terminated at Compton, and it is noted that "it is 10 miles long and falls 300 feet from the Cromford and High Peak Railway with nearly an uniform inclination."

The alternative route "shews a Line surveyed to terminate at Ashbourn Green, it has a fall of 65 feet in the first 3½ miles from the North East End then descends into the Valley by an inclined Plane 440 yds long, falling 100 feet, & afterwards has an uniform Descent of 21 feet in a mile, total length of this Line being 9 miles."

It is intriguing some 150 years later to compare the original sketch map with the 1:25000 Ordnance Survey maps for the area, and to note the correspondence of wooded areas like Hall Wood & Big Covert. The inclined plane would have had a gradient of about 1 in 13 and one must assume it would have been rope worked on similar principles to those on the High Peak line. It would have brought the railway down to run alongside Stow Brook, not far from Oldfield Lane Bridge. Both routes were close to one another to the top of the incline, at which point the Compton line took a more southerly, but roughly parallel course higher on the side of the valley, the two diverging to their respective termini after passing Agnes Meadow, at which point there was a limeworks when Mr Woodhouse carried out his survey.

The Middleton Incline, with a gradient of 1 in 8¼, is 708 yards in

op: No. 47000 seen here attached o the haulage rope for descent f the Middleton Incline in 1955.
Author's Collection

Middle: About to descend!
Author's Collection

Bottom: No. 41536 nearing Middleton Top after interchange vith No. 47000, having been vorking the Sheep Pasture Top o Middleton Bottom section of he line, while No. 47000 was ndergoing repairs in 1955.
Author's Collection

With Derbyshire County Council P.O. wagons awaiting movement, this view shows the dramatic angle change to the trackwork on Middleton Incline in May 1934.

H.C. Casserley

A further view of No. 7527 hauling nine open wagons nearing the top of Hopton Incline in May 1934.

H.C. Casserley

NLR locomotive 0–6–0T No. 58860 in early BR days climbing Hopton Incline with two water tenders. *LGRP, Courtesy David and Charles*

Hopton Top to Friden train arriving at Longcliffe. *LGRP, Courtesy David and Charles*

length. By far the most interesting feature at Middleton is the winding engine, which is the sole survivor of eight which were provided between 1825 and 1829. The records state that this engine was built in 1825 by the Butterley Iron Works, of Butterley, Derbyshire. The engine is of the two-cylinder low-pressure condensing beam type, steam distribution being effected by slide valves, operated by fixed eccentrics, making the engine non-reversing. It is possible to move the valves by hand to facilitate starting. The cylinders are 25 in. bore by 60 in. stroke, and steam is supplied at a pressure of five pounds per square inch by two wood-fired Lancashire boilers. The original feed pumps are still in use, and the fuel for the boilers is provided by the Carriage and Wagon Works at Derby, who despatch two wagon loads every weekday for the purpose. The drive from the engine to the rope pulleys is by a single reduction gear wheel and pinion, with a ratio of 2.75 to 1. The pinion is secured to the engine crankshaft and has a pitch diameter of 5 ft. The driving gear, to which the driving pulley is attached, has a pitch diameter of 13 ft 9½ in. The cast-iron flywheel, which has a sectional rim, is also approximately 14 ft in diameter. Working of the incline is similar to that at Sheep Pasture, except that there is no catch pit. Bell and pointer signals, transmitted by wires, are used between the Bottom and the Top.

There was a period between 1856 and 1894 when Middleton Incline was worked as a single line, because one line had been connected by a siding to a quarry which had been opened part way down the incline. This quarry did not operate for very long, being recorded as "long out of use in 1865", so it is perhaps surprising that it took so long to restore the two-track operation, which came back into operation on 2 April 1894.

Although not strictly connected with the incline, the corrugated-iron locomotive shed at Middleton Top has a peculiar feature, in that any water which drains into the pit runs into the nearby reservoir, from where it is pumped by the winding engine, which also performs this duty, into a suitable water tank. This economy is necessary because all water for locomotive purposes, and also for the stationary engines, has to be brought in tanks from Cromford Wharf. The supply comes from a spring in the hillside above Cromford Wharf, and the travelling tanks are converted from ex-LNWR tenders. Besides providing water for the engines and locomotives at Sheep Pasture Top, Middleton Top, and Longcliffe Goods, these tanks also provide homesteads with their domestic supply at various points. There are 21 rail tanks all told, some of which are converted from McConnell four-wheeled tenders built at Wolverton between 1851 and 1863, and the rest are six-wheelers of the Ramsbottom or Webb periods. Cromford despatches about 100 tanks of water a month for use along the line.

From Middleton Top the line rises gently all the way to the bottom of the Hopton Incline. A short distance from Middleton, a siding diverging to the right serves the Prestwich Intake Quarry, which is of considerable extent. The railway company (now the British Transport Commission) has a contract with this firm to provide 1,000 gallons of water per day for quarry purposes; this is brought in the travelling water tanks. After passing the quarry, the track plunges into the damp, unlined limestone bore of Hopton Tunnel, 113 yards long. Upon emerging, the driver can see ahead of him Hopton, whose chief claim to fame is that it is by far the steepest gradient worked by adhesion locomotives in the British Isles today. A matter of 457 yards in length, it rises with successive gradients of 1 in 60, 1 in 30, and 1 in 20, followed by a pitch of 1 in 14 for 200 yards, which eases to 1 in 470 just before reaching the top.

When the line was opened, Hopton was worked as a stationary engine operated incline in the same manner as the others, and it continued in this manner until 1877. Hopton Incline, along with that at Whaley Bridge, shared the distinction of having used chains for haulage throughout their working lives. When the stationary engine was in use, the whole length of the incline was pitched at 1 in 14, and two sets of metals were provided. Today, only a single track exists, and the only sign of the winding engine house is a mound at the side of the line where this building once stood. The Hopton engine was similar to the Middleton engine, being constructed by the Butterley Company about the same time. The working pressure was lower, however, being only 2½ pounds per square inch; this was lowered to 1½ pounds before the engine finished work.

Before 1877 an attempt had been made to operate the incline with a special locomotive, built by Fox, Walker & Co. (later Peckett's) of Bristol, and incorporating the Handyside system for operating on steep gradients. This remarkable machine was similar to a normal railway locomotive, except that the frames at the trailing end were strengthened to support a winding drum on which was wound a coil of wire rope. This drum was driven through gears from a separate set of cylinders and crankshaft, and at the end of the hauling rope was a special truck, which could be clipped to the rails. The locomotive itself was provided with a similar set of clips for the same purpose. When a load was to be hauled up the incline, the wagons, limited to two in number, were

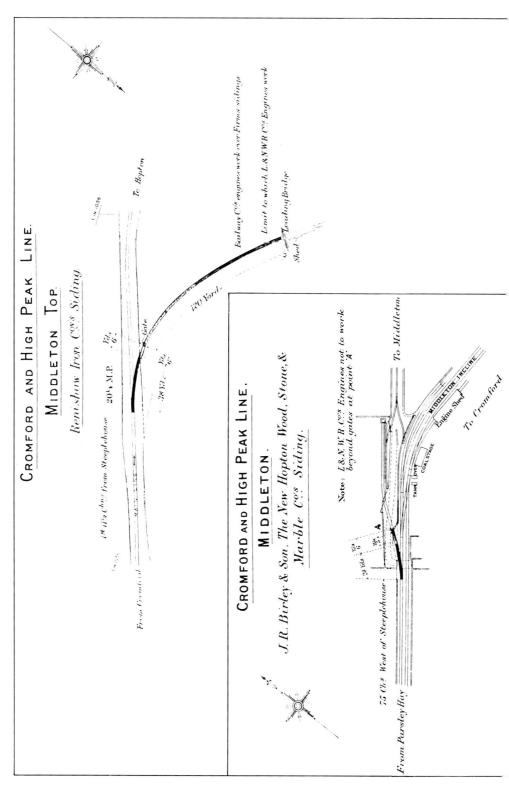

CROMFORD AND HIGH PEAK LINE.

MIDDLETON TOP.

Renishaw Iron Co's Siding.

1ᵐ 4½ chns from Steeplehouse 20⁴ M.P.

Vₛ 6'.

Rₛ Wₛ Vₛ 6'.

From Cromford

Gate

To Hopton

1ᵐ 10.56

Railway Co's engines work over Firms sidings

Limit to which L&NWR Co's Engines work

120 Yards.

Loading Bridge

Shed

CROMFORD AND HIGH PEAK LINE.

MIDDLETON.

J. R. Birley & Son, The New Hopton Wood, Stone, & Marble Co's Siding.

Note: L&N.W.R Co's Engines not to work beyond gates at point 'A'.

To Middleton

MIDDLETON INCLINE

Engine Shed

To Cromford

COALSTAGE

TANK

OVER

A

Vₛ 6'.

Vₛ 6'.

55 Chs West of Steeplehouse

From Parsley Hay

up or down the Inclined Planes, and all passengers to be compelled to wait till the descending Train is in motion before they proceed to walk down such Inclined Plane; and the ascending Train not to be drawn up until all the passengers have arrived at the top.

32. Not more than two loaded Trucks are to be hung on at one time, either for ascent or descent, or a greater gross weight than 2½ tons, each truck having a separate tail chain fastening.

33. The number of small loaded Waggons hung on for descent at one time must not exceed three, or a gross weight of 18 tons, each waggon having a separate tail chain fastening.

34. In no instance whatever must any Waggons be coupled with the two Fly Waggons, either in ascending or descending any of the Inclined Planes.

35. The number of empty Trucks ascending shall not exceed two, or a gross weight of 8 tons.

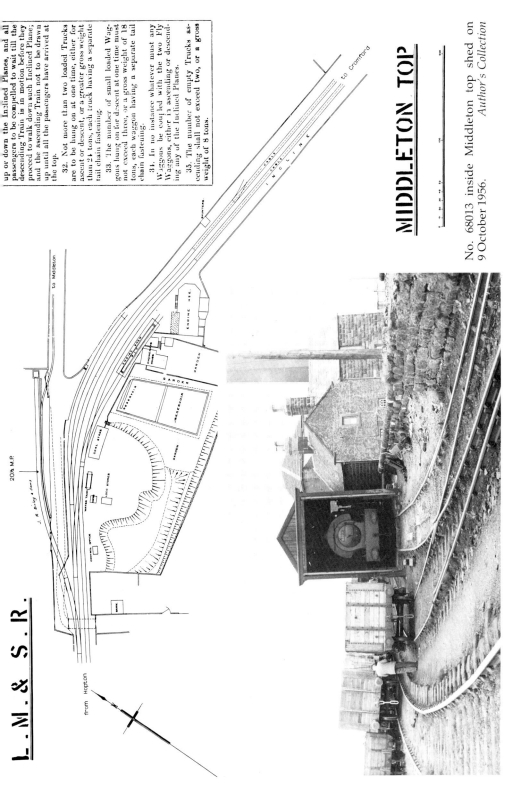

20½ M.P.

J. R. Billig & Sons

to Middleton

from Hopton

L. M. & S. R.

ENGINE SHED

GARDEN

COAL STAGE

WATER TANK

LOCO STORES

CONTROL OFFICE

WEIGHBRIDGE

CABLE DUCT

CABLE INCLINE

JUNCTION

to Cromford

MIDDLETON TOP

No. 68013 inside Middleton top shed on 9 October 1956.
Author's Collection

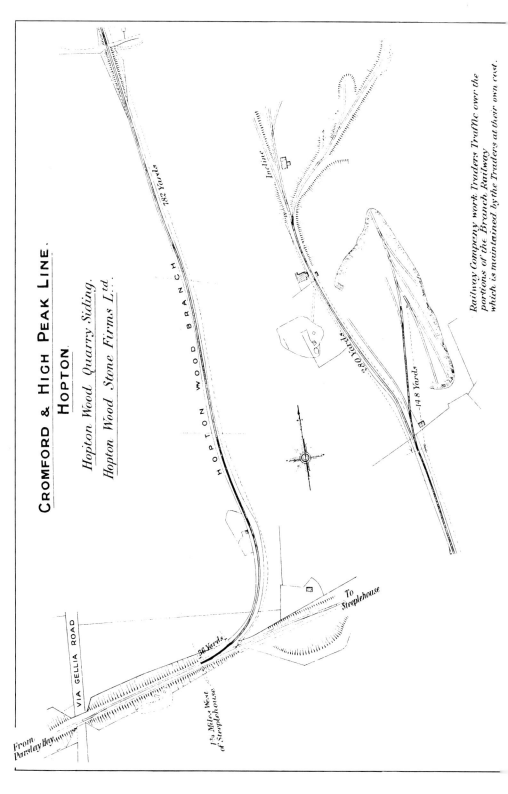

CROMFORD & HIGH PEAK LINE.

HOPTON.

Hopton Wood Quarry Siding.

Hopton Wood Stone Firms L^{td}.

Railway Company work Traders Traffic over the portions of the Branch Railway which is maintained by the Traders at their own cost.

782 Yards

HOPTON WOOD BRANCH

Incline

308 Yards

148 Yards

VIA GELLIA ROAD

36 Yards

To Steeplehouse

1¼ Miles West of Steeplehouse

From Parsley Hay

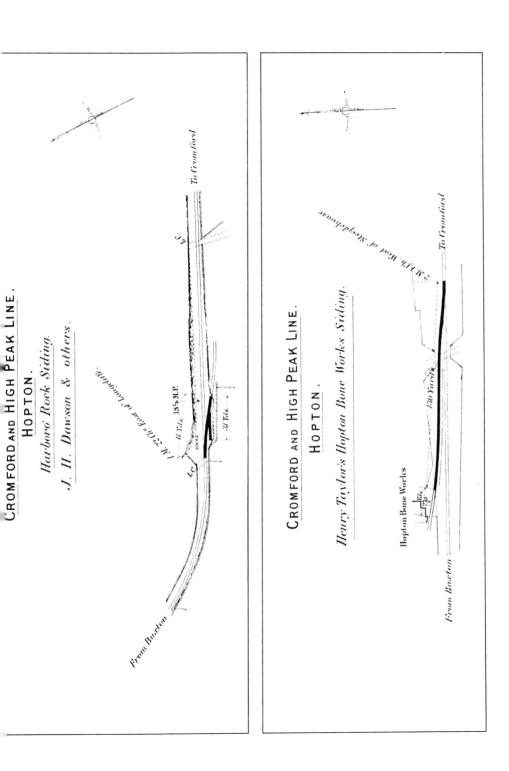

CROMFORD AND HIGH PEAK LINE.

HOPTON.

Harboro' Rock Siding.

J. H. Dawson & others.

To Cromford

From Buxton

CROMFORD AND HIGH PEAK LINE.

HOPTON.

Henry Taylor's Hopton Bone Works Siding.

To Cromford

Hopton Bone Works

From Buxton

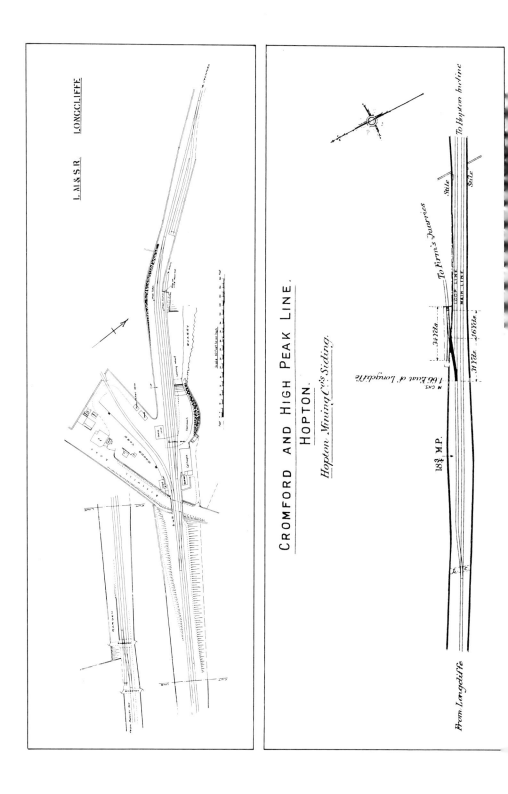

L.M.&.S.R   LONGCLIFFE

CROMFORD AND HIGH PEAK LINE.

HOPTON.

Hopton Mining Co.'s Siding.

The summit of Hopton Incline on the line, seen here in May 1934, showing well the gradient change! *H.C. Casserley*

Ascending in style the Hopton Incline with No. 7527 under full pressure on 4 May 1934. *H.C. Casserley*

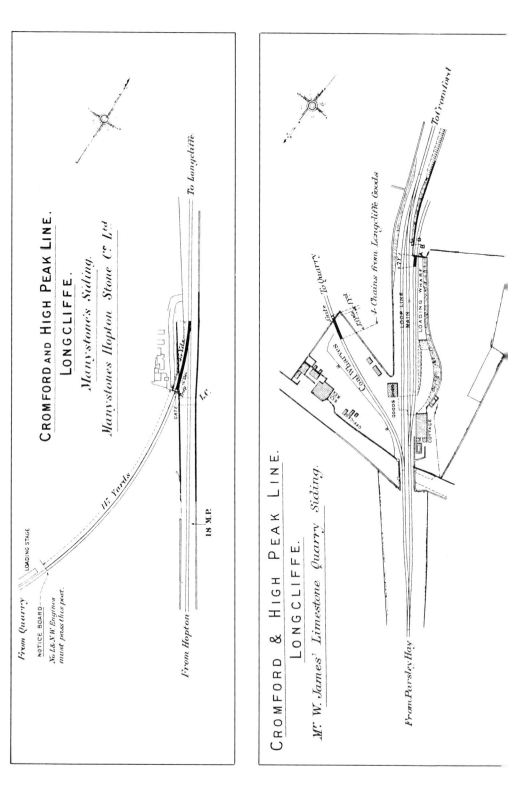

CROMFORD AND HIGH PEAK LINE.
LONGCLIFFE.
Manystone's Siding.
Manystones Hopton Stone Co. Ltd.

From Quarry

LOADING STAGE

NOTICE BOARD

No L&NW Engines must pass this post.

147 Yards

To Longcliffe

GATE

LC.

18 M.P.

From Hopton

CROMFORD & HIGH PEAK LINE.
LONGCLIFFE.
Mr. W. James' Limestone Quarry Siding.

From Parsley Hay

To Cromford

4 Chains from Longcliffe Goods

Gate to Quarry

(Coal) Wharves

LOOP LINE

MAIN

LOADING WHARF

GOODS

OFFICE

COTTAGE

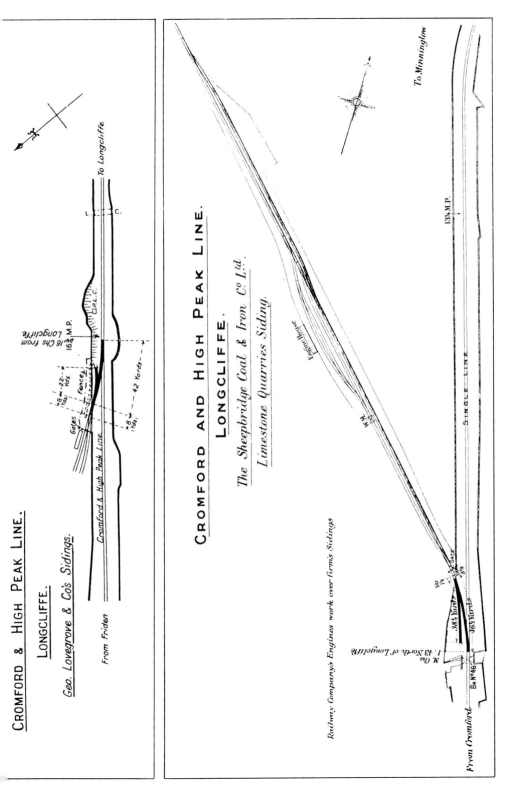

CROMFORD & HIGH PEAK LINE.

LONGCLIFFE.

Geo. Lovegrove & Co's Sidings.

To Longcliffe

L.   C.

D.L.C.

16¾ M.P.
16 Chs from
Longcliffe

Gates

Fence

22 Yds

8 Yds

8 Yds

42 Yards

Cromford & High Peak Line

From Friden

CROMFORD AND HIGH PEAK LINE.

LONGCLIFFE.

The Sheepbridge Coal & Iron Co Ld.

Limestone Quarries Siding.

To Minninglow

13¾ M.P.

SINGLE LINE

Engine House

W.M.

Railway Company's Engines work over firm's Sidings

GATE

8¼

Yd

1.13

38¾ Yards

46¾ Yards

M. Chs
1.13 North of Longcliffe

Br No 46

From Cromford

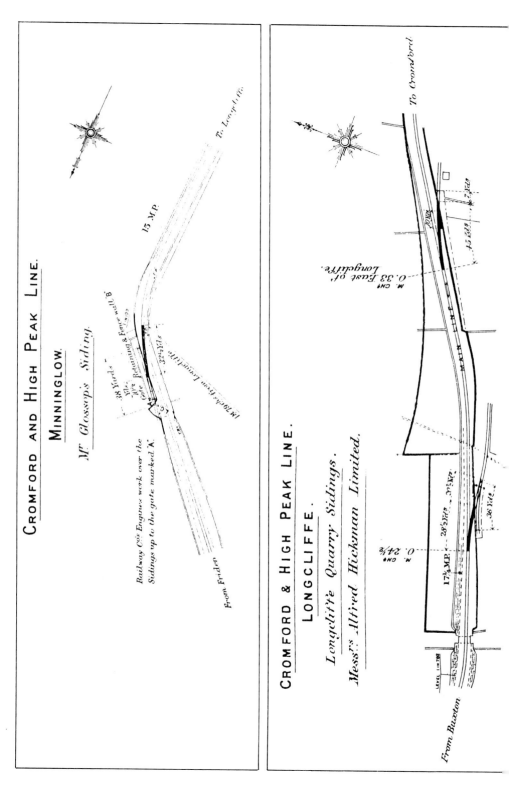

CROMFORD AND HIGH PEAK LINE.

MINNINGLOW.

Mr Glossop's Siding.

15 M.P.

To Longcliffe

28 Yards

Retaining & Fence wall "B"

Gate up to the gate marked "A".

[1879] from Longcliffe

34 Yards

Railway C^{os} Engines work over the
Sidings up to the gate marked "A".

From Friden

CROMFORD & HIGH PEAK LINE.

LONGCLIFFE.

Longcliffe Quarry Sidings.

Messrs Alfred Hickman Limited.

To Cromford

0.33 East of
Longcliffe

M. CH^s

45 Yds

7 Yds

17¾ M.P.   0. 24½
M. CH^s

28 Yards   3½ Yds

36 Yds

LEVEL

From Buxton

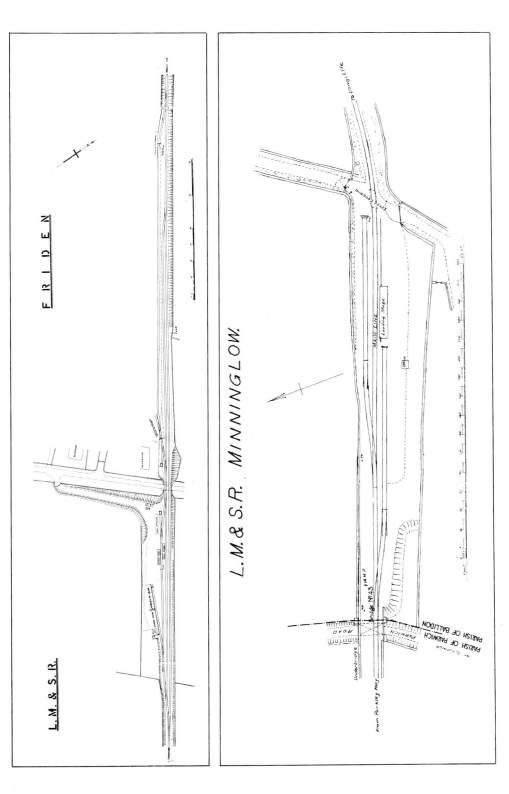

FRIDEN

L.M. & S.R.

L.M. & S.R. MINNINGLOW.

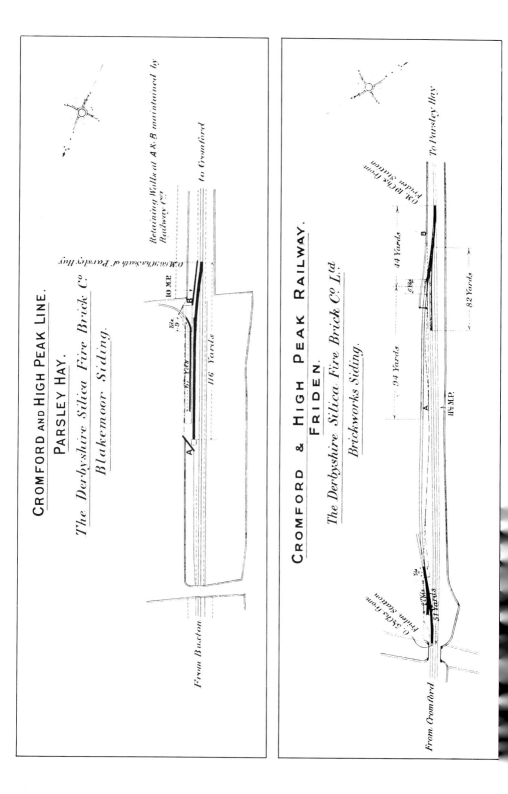

CROMFORD AND HIGH PEAK LINE.

PARSLEY HAY.

The Derbyshire Silica Fire Brick Cº

Blakemoor Siding.

CROMFORD & HIGH PEAK RAILWAY.

FRIDEN.

The Derbyshire Silica Fire Brick Cº Ltd.

Brickworks Siding.

Parsley Hay Station looking towards Buxton. The points give access to the yard on the right. The junction with the High Peak line is at the other end of the station (behind the photographer). Note the wooden platform construction.

LGRP, Courtesy David and Charles

Enthusiasts special made up of open wagons and brake vans standing at Parsley Hay.

LGRP, Courtesy David and Charles

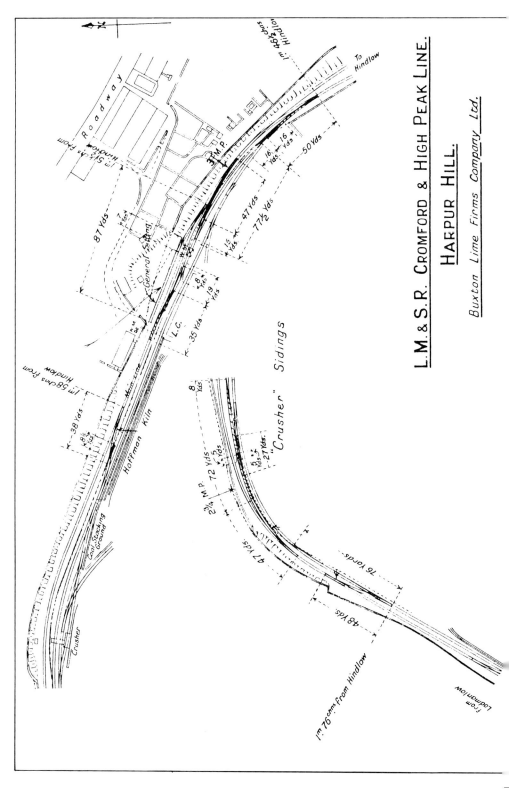

L.M. & S.R. Cromford & High Peak Line.

Harpur Hill.

Buxton Lime Firms Company Ltd.

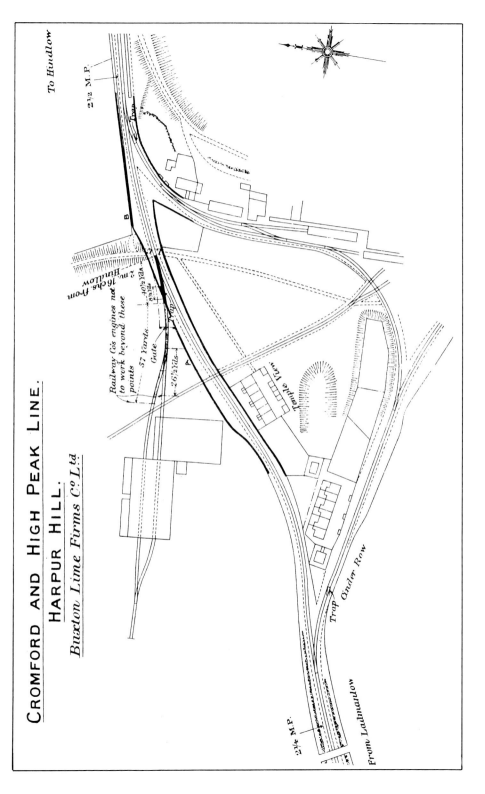

CROMFORD AND HIGH PEAK LINE.
HARPUR HILL.
Buxton Lime Firms Cº Ltd.

To Hindlow

2½ M.P.

Trap

B

2 m. 16 chs. from Hindlow

Railway Cºs engines not to work beyond these points

40½ Yds.
8¾ Yds.

57 Yards
Gate
Trap

26½ Yds.

A

Temple View

2¼ M.P.

Trap   Onder Row

From Ladmanlow

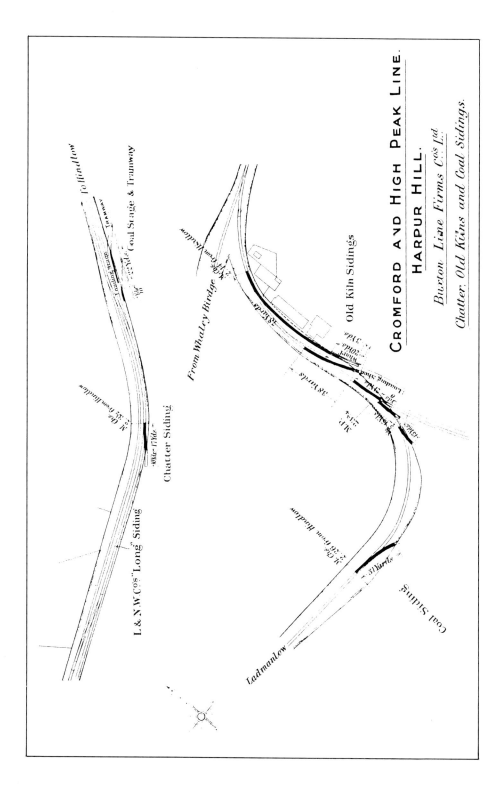

CROMFORD AND HIGH PEAK LINE.

HARPUR HILL.

Buxton Lime Firms Cᵒˢ Lᵗᵈ

Chatter, Old Kilns and Coal Sidings.

Tollhadlow

TRAMWAY

2 Yds Coal Stage & Tramway

Loading Siding

From Whaley Birdge

Old Kiln Sidings

48 Yards

38 Yards

Loading Shed

From Ladmanlow

Chatter Siding

M Cᵒˢ from Hindlow

40He 17Yds

L & N.W Cᵒˢ "Long" Siding

Ladmanlow

M Cᵒˢ from Hindlow

Coal Sidings

30 Yards

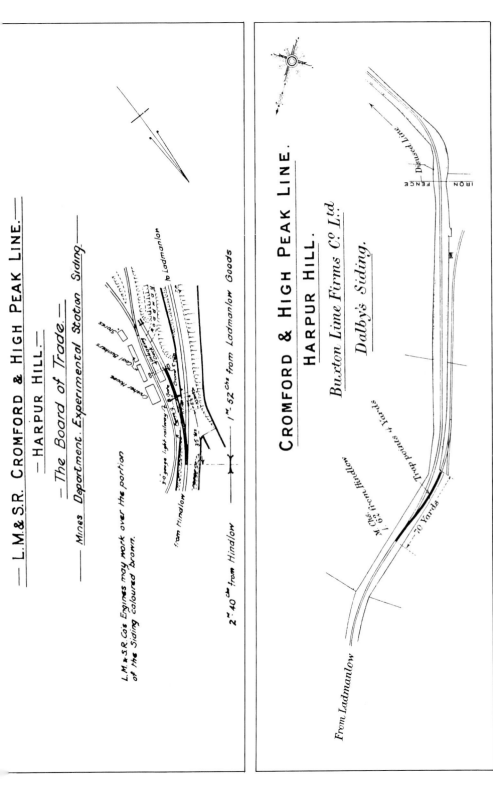

L.M.&S.R. CROMFORD & HIGH PEAK LINE.
— HARPUR HILL. —
— The Board of Trade. —
— Mines Department. Experimental Station Siding —

L.M.&S.R. Co's Engines may work over the portion of the Siding coloured brown.

to Ladmanlow

Coal House

Coal Bunkers

Spares

2'-0" gauge light railway

35 yds

from Hindlow

to Ladmanlow Goods

1 M. 52 Chs from Ladmanlow Goods

2 M. 40 Chs from Hindlow

CROMFORD & HIGH PEAK LINE.
— HARPUR HILL. —
Buxton Lime Firms Co. Ltd.
Dalby's Siding.

From Ladmanlow

1 M. Chs. from Hindlow
6½

Trap points 4 Yards

70 Yards

IRON FENCE

Disused Lead Line

coupled to the special truck. The locomotive then proceeded up the incline, paying out the wire rope as it went. When all the rope was unwound, the locomotive was clipped down to the track, and the winding engine was started up. The special truck, trailing the loaded wagons, was hauled up to where the locomotive was standing, and the truck was clipped. After releasing its clips, the locomotive then climbed to the top of the incline, the length of the wire rope being sufficient to enable this to be done in two stages. After securing the locomotive again, and taking up the slack in the rope, the truck was freed, and the wagons hauled up to the top. It is not certain whether the reverse of the process was employed for wagons going down the incline, or whether these were coupled to the locomotive with the brakes fastened down, as is the case today. As can be imagined, the operation was very tedious, and it was found that a locomotive with two or three wagons trailing could reach the top of the incline, provided a reasonable run could be taken at it.

Locomotive working began on 16 April 1877, after the gradients had been modified, and this method is at present in use. Two ex-North London Railway 0–6–0 tanks, sub-shedded at Middleton Top from Rowsley, share in this arduous task. The load for these engines is 5 full wagons or 7 empties, going up, but no limit is prescribed when coming down from the Top, provided all brakes are pinned down hard. One of the North London engines, then numbered 27521, was involved in an accident on the approach to Hopton Incline on 6 October 1937, when the 8.35 am Middleton Top to Parsley Hay freight became derailed, resulting in four wagons and the locomotive rolling down an embankment on to the road, which runs parallel to the railway at this point. Unfortunately the driver, Mr Boden, was fatally injured, and the fireman, shunter and guard had to jump for their lives. The official enquiry disclosed that high-speed tactics were being employed; this had caused excessive nosing by the locomotive, spreading the track and derailing the train. Since that time, a limit of 40 miles per hour has been enforced on the curve approaching the bottom of the incline. The first train of the day, which is sometimes rather heavy, from Middleton is booked for "assistance to Hopton Top", and so the North London engines are used to double-head the train on its one-and-a-half mile journey. One engine then takes the train forward to Longcliffe and Friden, where an ex-Midland 0–6–0 takes over, while the other shunts at Hopton Top and then returns to Middleton, picking up wagons from quarries as required.

The line, in avoiding engineering works of any size, abounds in sharp curves, and on the section between Longcliffe Goods and Friden there are twenty-one curves of five chains radius or less, three of these being only three chains, and one, the well-known Gotham Curve, only 2½ chains in radius, turns the line through 80 degrees. This, of course, is the reason that only four-wheeled wagons are permitted south of Friden, and even these grind and groan as they are pulled slowly round the curves. Gotham Curve has been stated to have had no fewer than 11 in. superelevation at one time, while another source claimed that the superelevation was 5½ in. and a check rail was provided. Early photographs at the curve certainly show that there was considerable superelevation; a visit in 1954 revealed no difference in height, although the expected check rail was all-present-and-correct.

In the 33 miles of the original line there were four tunnels. These were, from south to north, Hopton, Newhaven Road, Hindlow, and Burbage; the first three of these are still in use. Hopton Tunnel, which precedes the curve approaching the bottom of the Hopton Incline, has already been mentioned. It is approached at each end by deep limestone cuttings.

Newhaven Road Tunnel carries the main Ashbourne to Buxton road over the railway. It is only 51 yards in length but it is particularly interesting by virtue of the carved stone blocks incorporated in the facings above the north and south portals. The block facing south depicts a crude wagon, surrounded by the words "Cromford and High Peak Railway 1825", the four corners of the tablet bearing the letters "P.H. & Co.", these being the initials of the contractor Hargreaves who was responsible for this section. Above the north mouth of the tunnel the crest of the company appears. This was in the form of a four-wheeled wagon on a shield over the motto "Divina Palladis Arte", with a garter surrounding the whole, inscribed "Cromford and High Peak Railway Comp'y. Incorporated 1825". Above this block is another bearing the inscription "Jos[s]. Jessop Esqr. Engineer". The phrase "Divina Palladis Arte" when translated means "By the Divine skill of Pallas" (or Minerva, being the goddess of knowledge and science).

The last of the three tunnels which are in use is the 514-yard Hindlow Tunnel. This is on the Ashbourne to Buxton line and is double tracked, both of the tunnels mentioned earlier being bored for one line only. The course of the old line, abandoned in 1892, runs at right angles across the present line, above the north portal of Hindlow Tunnel.

The longest tunnel on the original line was the now-disused Burbage Tunnel, which bored its way through 580 yards of rock,

L.M.S. Cromford & High Peak Line.

Ladmanlow

Clay Cross Company Ltd.
Grinn Branch Siding.

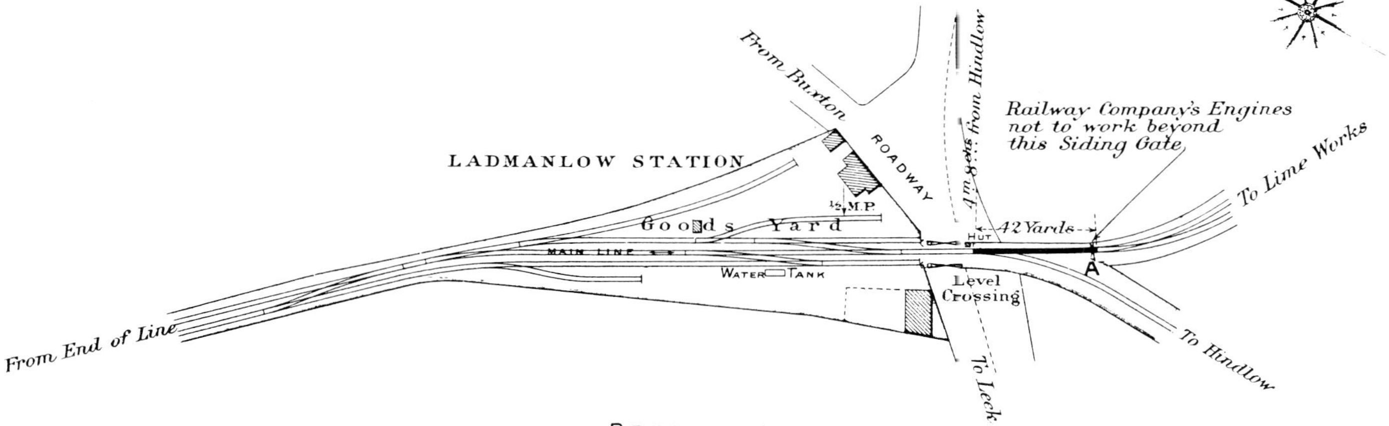

TO 1924.

To Line Works

To Hindlow

Railway Company's Engines
not to work beyond
this Siding Gate.

42 Yards

1 in 8 ins from Hindlow

Level Crossing

To Leck

From Buxton

ROADWAY

½ MP

Goods Yard

LADMANLOW STATION

WATER TANK

MAIN LINE

From End of Line

REFERENCE

42 Yards and Gate maintained by Railway Company on own land at own cost.
Traders pay cost of renewing & maintaining Signals in connection with Siding.
See Agreement with The Clay Cross Co. Ltd., dated 12th April 1924.

Ladmanlow Yard looking towards Whaley Bridge in LMS days. Crossing the line, in the foreground, is the Buxton to Leek road. *LGRP, Courtesy David and Charles*

A view looking in the opposite direction showing the signal post seen on *page 17*. *LGRP, Courtesy David and Charles*

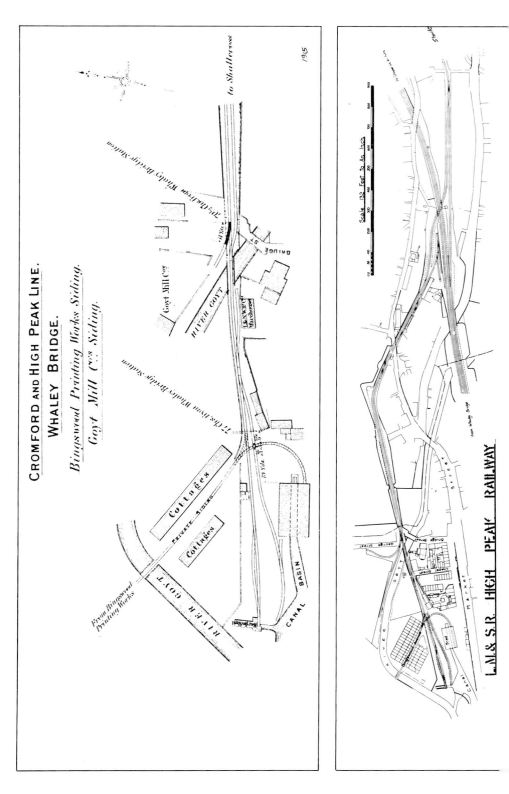

CROMFORD AND HIGH PEAK LINE.
WHALEY BRIDGE.

Bingswood Printing Works Siding.
Goyt Mill C⁰ˢ Siding.

Cottages

Cottages

PRIVATE SIDING

RIVER GOYT

From Bingswood Printing Works

CANAL

BASIN

77 Chs. from Whaley Bridge Station

70 Chs. from Whaley Bridge Station

RIVER GOYT

Goyt Mill C⁰

R.M.W.W Warehouse

BRIDGE

to Shallcross

195

Scale 132 Feet to an Inch

George Street

Bridge Street

Canal Street

Market Street

RIVER GOYT

CANAL

from Whaley Bridge

L.M.& S.R. HIGH PEAK RAILWAY

on the Ladmanlow to Shallcross section; this was abandoned in 1892. A recent visit showed that brick walls had been built about 20 yards inside the tunnel at each end, and in addition, a wooden screen trimmed with barbed wire had been erected at the south end. The stonework at this end was in a good state of preservation considering its sixty-odd years of disuse, but the northern portal was crumbling, and a heap of fallen stonework showed where the ravages of time and weather had taken their toll.

Reference to the map of the line shows that it serves a large number of small sidings with long names, such as Hopton Wood Stone Firm's Middleton Branch, Lovegroves Longcliffe Limestone Siding, and Black Rocks Stone Company's Siding. Between Friden and Sheep Pasture Top there are more than fifteen sidings, most of which serve quarries, although one goes to the Derbyshire Silica Firebrick Company's Works near Friden, and another at the bottom of Hopton Incline is a siding which served a now-derelict bone manure works. There is also a yard at Middleton Bottom called Middle Peak Siding which meets the needs of Middleton village. One of the largest quarries served is at the top of the Hopton Wood Stone Firm's Branch; this has its own locomotive for internal traffic. This is an outside-cylinder 0–4–0 saddle tank built by Peckett of Bristol in 1924 (works No. 1669).

Further along the line, between Dowlow Halt and Ladmanlow, the line bristles with sidings. These serve more quarries and limeworks, a wagon repair works, the Ministry of Fuel and Power Safety in Mines Research Station, and a storage depot. Near Harpur Hill the Imperial Chemical Industries Hoffman Siding used to serve the Hoffman lime kiln, which was lit in 1875 and was demolished in 1952, after having been burning continuously for over 70 years.

Mention has already been made of the mobile water tanks used for supplies up and down the line. These provide water for domestic purposes at Hopton Top, Parsley Hay and Hurdlow, and at Hartington and Alsop-en-le-Dale on the Ashbourne to Buxton line. The usual practice is for the cottagers to fetch their water in buckets, which are placed under the injector feed pipe, and the valve opened to fill the bucket. At some points, such as Parsley Hay, the water is run into a tank from which it is drawn by a pump.

The remaining inclines of the High Peak Railway are all disused. Hurdlow Incline, which in the original line was 850 yards long and pitched at 1 in 16, was last worked on 2 January 1869, when it was replaced by the Hurdlow Deviation, with a maximum gradient of 1 in 60. The course of the original line is still quite plain, the walls on either side being in position, and an electric transmission line also follows the line of the old incline, which diverges sharply to the north-west at Hurdlow station, which was closed to all traffic in August 1949.

Bunsall Incline is one of the inclines on the section north of Ladmanlow which was abandoned on 25 June 1892, when the new line from Hurdlow to Buxton was opened. When it was opened, Bunsall was worked as two separate inclines, the upper one being 660 yards long, with a gradient of 1 in 7½, while the lower one was shorter, being 455 yards long, and somewhat steeper, at 1 in 7. Working as one incline began on 8 June 1857. Today Bunsall Incline is plainly visible, as is most of the abandoned section. The Derbyshire dry stone walls are falling down in parts; sheep roam where trucks used to rattle up and down, and all that remains of the winding engine house are two crumbling walls and a pile of moss-covered stones. The incline is covered with short springy moorland turf, through which protrude the original stone blocks which were the foundations of the stops used to prevent the wagons running down the incline. From the top of Bunsall Incline there is an impressive view of the Goyt Valley, with the Goyt reservoir far below, alongside which runs the course of the Cromford & High Peak Railway on its way from the bottom of Bunsall Incline through Fernilee to Shallcross.

Shallcross Incline was not so steep as some of the others, being graded at 1 in 10¼. It was 817 yards in length, and the bottom of the incline was not very far from Whaley Bridge. Today the upper parts of the incline have been built over by a new housing estate, while the remainder is either densely overgrown or occupied by a series of hen houses. At the bottom of the incline is Shallcross Yard, which is still used by British Railways, being reached by a spur from the Whaley Bridge and Buxton line, which was opened on 17 August 1857 (see page 14).

The remaining incline, Whaley Bridge, is actually situated in the town itself. It was last used on 9 April 1952 and right down to that time was worked by horses. Approach to the incline is under a very low bridge, so that wagons had to be hauled to and from the top of the incline by this same means, as the clearance was not sufficient to permit locomotives to pass. The incline is now very much overgrown, particularly round the old capstan by which the chains were driven to move the wagons up and down the incline. The horse was harnessed to one end of a wooden beam which was bolted to the top of a vertical spindle which disappeared into a pit

Whaley Bridge. This low bridge under the Whaley to Buxton line prevented wagons being shunted from Shallcross Yard to and from the incline, except by horses. Connection from the main line to Shallcross yard is on the left.　　*LGRP, Courtesy David and Charles*

A fine view of Whaley Bridge Incline. The horse operated winch is unfortunately out of view in this photograph being just to the left of the sloping roofed building seen in the foreground.　　*LGRP, Courtesy David and Charles*

Whaley Bridge Transit Shed situated on the Peak Canal showing the railway doors on either side of the canal basin (centre). The furthest door seems now to be used by the START MOTOR CO.! *LGRP, Courtesy David and Charles*

Shallcross, showing the track winding through the houses from Shallcross yard towards Whaley Bridge. *LGRP, Courtesy David and Charles*

covered with boards. The lower end of the spindle was fitted with a pinion which engaged a large gear wheel, which drove the horizontal pulley round which the chain passed. A similar loose pulley in a covered pit at the bottom of the incline was used to carry the chain from one track to the other. The Whaley Bridge Incline was much shorter than all the rest, being only 180 yards long and rising at 1 in 13½. At the bottom of the incline, the tracks ran to a wharf alongside the Peak Forest Canal and into a couple of mills. When the incline was in use, this section was also worked by horses.

Oddments in the workshops at Cromford including a section of cast iron fish-bellied rail.   *Author's Collection*

Chapter 3
Motive Power

Although the horse was the prime mover on the Cromford &
High Peak Railway when the line was first opened, it was only a
few years before the company began to think in terms of steam
locomotives. Unfortunately, information on the early stock is
rather meagre, and some conflicting evidence exists.

The first steam locomotive to run on the line, numbered "1",
appears to have been built by Robert Stephenson and Co. of
Newcastle, in 1833. This was an 0–4–0, with 5ft wheels and 12in.
by 16in. cylinders. It bore the works No. 45, and also carried the
name *Peak*. After May 1863 it seems to have been employed "in the
workshop" at Cromford Wharf, presumably as a stationary engine.
It was disposed of before 1871, when the London & North Western
Railway took over the locomotive stock.

No. 2 was a 2–2–0 tender engine built by E. Bury and delivered
in 1835. It had 12in. by 18in. cylinders driving 4ft 8in. diameter
wheels; the leading wheels were 3ft in diameter. Measuring with
its tender 32ft 3in. long, it weighed 9tons 10cwts. In November
1871 it became LNWR 2039 and the next month LNWR 1942. By
May 1873 it had been rebuilt at Crewe into a 2–2–0 saddle tank and
lettered "B", for shunting at Crewe.

Some doubt exists about locomotive No. 3, but it seems likely
that this was an 0–6–0 built by the Vulcan Foundry (then
Tayleur's) of Newton-le-Willows in 1842. It bore the works No. 175
and had 5ft driving wheels and 14in. by 20in. cylinders. No
further information is available.

After the arrival of No. 3, no further locomotives are shown in
the stock list until 1859, when two were built by the company in
their own workshops at Cromford. The term "built" should be
interpreted rather freely, as it seems unlikely that the "building"
could have been more than a putting together of parts. It is known
that around 1840 the railway company were buying locomotive
parts from Falconer and Peach, Union Foundry, Derby. Exactly
which locomotive or locomotives these items were for is open to
conjecture. In February 1841, John Leonard, who was the C&HPR
resident engineer, was reported in the *Derby Mercury* as having
designed and built an outside-cylinder locomotive, and that this
had been tried out; it was intended to build two more. By the
following year, two locomotives had been built, but it is not known
whether these were additional to the one mentioned above, or if
that was one of the pair. The name *Pioneer* was carried by one of
these engines, but whether they were ever entered into the stock

An LNWR Allan "Crewe Goods" 2–4–0 posing on Gotham curve with an assortment of freight wagons.
LGRP, Courtesy David and Charles

LNWR 2–4–0T No. 3049 near the top of the Hopton Incline. Note the "Fly" passenger coach at the rear and that both tracks existed when this early view was taken.
LGRP, Courtesy David and Charles

Example of advert in *The Engineer* in 1876 showing the Handyside Steep Gradient Company's Locomotive which is reputed to have been demonstrated on the Hopton Incline. The principle used was that the locomotive gripped the rails and hauled wagons up the incline by steam winch.

Peak Park Planning Board & Derbyshire County Council

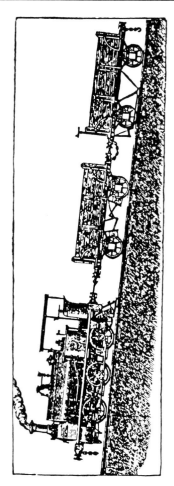

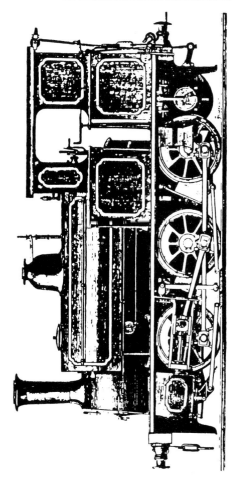

HANDYSIDE'S
STEEP
GRADIENT
SYSTEM

May be Seen at Work on the Hopton Incline Section of the
High Peak Railway,

BY THE KIND PERMISSION OF THE

LONDON & NORTH-WESTERN
RAILWAY COMPANY,

The Incline is **1** in **14**, and the Weight (including Engine) taken UP is **70** TONS, and DOWN **164** TONS. All the traffic on this section of the Railway is now worked by One Small PATENT LOCOMOTIVE.

PERSONS DESIRING TO SEE THE ABOVE ARE INVITED TO DO SO AND MAY ADDRESS FOR FURTHER INFORMATION.

HENRY HANDYSIDE, ESQ.,
RED LION HOTEL
WIRKSWORTH, DERBYSHIRE.

The Incline may be reached from Matlock Bath, by carriage, the distance being about 4 miles and from Wirksworth distance about 1½ miles

list is uncertain; so is their ultimate fate.

It was, however, 1859 before any more locomotives appeared in the stock list. These were Nos. 4 and 5, 0–6–0 tanks, with 3 ft wheels and 10 in. by 12 in. cylinders, weighing 12 tons 15 cwts. After the LNWR took over the stock in 1871, No. 4 became 2040 in November and 1943 a month later. In March 1877 it became "D" on the Locomotive Machinery Department list and survived until May 1882. No. 5 had a similar fate, becoming 2041 and 1944 at the same dates as No. 4, and was lettered "C" in the LMD in November 1876. Its date of scrapping is not known.

In 1860 the Vulcan Foundry delivered C&HPR Nos. 6 and 7. With Vulcan works Nos. 435 and 436, these were 0–6–0 saddle tanks, with 9 in. by 15 in. outside cylinders driving 3 ft coupled wheels, and a wheelbase of 8 ft 6 in. The middle driving wheels were without flanges. The boiler was pressed to 100 lb. per sq. in. and had a total heating surface of 274¼ sq. ft, made up of 240¼ sq. ft to the tubes and the remaining 34 sq. ft in the firebox. The grate area was 6.32 sq. ft, the weight 14 tons 9 cwt, and the overall length 21 ft 8 in. No. 6 arrived at Ladmanlow on 21 March and No. 7 in the next month. In November 1871 they became LNWR 2042/3, and 1945/6 in the duplicate list in December. No. 6 was scrapped in 1879; in March of the same year the former No. 7 had become Locomotive Machinery Department "F", finally being sold to a Mr Peak of Tunstall in the following November.

This completes the locomotive stock list of the Cromford & High Peak Railway Company as such. Before going on to look at some of the locomotives provided by the LNWR to work the line, reference must be made to an engine for which an order was placed with Neilson and Co. in March 1857. This appears to have been an 0–6–0 saddle tank, with 8 in. by 16 in. cylinders and wheels 3 ft 10 in. in diameter. Some authorities state that this locomotive was numbered "3"; if this was so, then presumably it was to replace the earlier Vulcan engine which bore that number. Unfortunately, the records concerning the locomotive or loco-motives carrying No. 3 are meagre in the extreme, and it is not possible to confirm this. The Neilson engine does not appear to have been suitable for working on the line, as by the end of July 1857 the builders had agreed to take back the new engine "upon receiving order for two others of less power and lighter weight". What actually took place is not known.

When the LNWR took over the working of the line in April 1861, a motley collection of power appeared and disappeared to supple-ment the C&HPR engines. These saw service until 1871, when, the

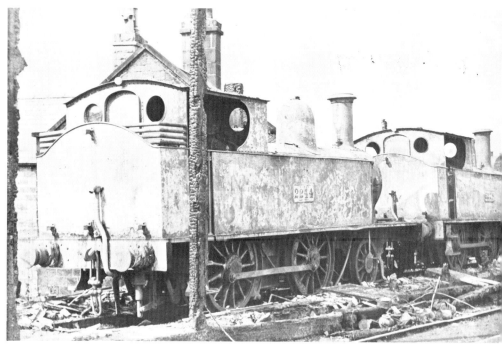

LNWR 2–4–0T locomotives Nos 2244 and 2278 seen here in a sorry state after a roasting when the Middleton locomotive shed burnt down in 1906.

LGRP, Courtesy David and Charles

The "Chopper" tank in British Rail livery showing the pop safety valves and sporting a 17D Rowsley shed plate on the smokebox door. *LGRP, Courtesy David and Charles*

A North London Railway 0–6–0T No. 27527 in LMSR livery, shunting at Cromford Wharf alongside the canal bank. *LGRP, Courtesy David and Charles*

Another of the same class of locomotive, again at Cromford Wharf, carrying its new BR number, but still lettered LMS. This particular engine, ex-27530, retains the original NLR chimney. *LGRP, Courtesy David and Charles*

An interesting scene at Cromford Wharf with LNWR 0–4–2T "Bissel Truck" in LMS livery, No. 7861, shunting LMS wagons. *LGRP, Courtesy David and Charles*

LMS tank No. 6428 (Chopper) showing well the Ramsbottom safety valves on the boiler. *LGRP, Courtesy David and Charles*

With shed code 20 (Buxton) on the smokebox this ex-LNWR 2–4–0T, Webb design, No. 6422, awaits at the top of Sheep Pasture in May 1934. *H.C. Casserley*

No. 47000 0–4–0ST in British Railways livery standing at Middleton Bottom in April 1953. *R.M. Casserley*

record states, "the five remaining C&HP locomotives were with-drawn". These would be Nos. 2, 4, 5, 6 and 7. A complete list of the "intruders" which appeared after 1861 has been set down chrono-logically by Mr G.J. Aston in a paper read to the Stephenson Locomotive Society, together with notes on each of the loco-motives concerned, and the whole of this information has appeared in the Society's *Journal*.* Apart from the 2–4–0 "Crewe Goods" tender engines, there were some 2–2–2 tender engines, two of which had originally been built for the Birkenhead Railway. A 2–4–0 side tank, also constructed for that line, named *Zopyrus*, was another visitor, while an engine of the same type which had begun work on the Kendal & Windermere Railway also found its way to the Derbyshire Peak District. An 0–4–0 tank from the K&WR also ran on C&HPR metals, and a Well Tank of the same wheel arrangement, built by George England and Co. of Hatcham in 1857 for the Sandy & Potton Railway, spent a fortnight on the line in August 1863, proving itself to be unsuitable. This engine was the well-known *Shannon*, sold to the Wantage Tramway in 1878 and now preserved at the Great Western Society Railway Centre at Didcot. Other railways represented were the Cocker-mouth & Workington, whose No. 3, an 0–4–2 tank, arrived in 1867, and the St Helens Railway, from which three engines, one an 0–4–0 tender and the others 2–4–0 tender, spent some time on the line.

By about 1880 it appears that the bulk of the working was in the hands of the Crewe Goods and the later Goods Tanks. The tender engines were designed by Messrs Trevithick and Allan, and this led to a reference by David P. Carr in his "Sidelights on the Crom-ford and High Peak Railway".† Mr Carr had walked over much of the route of the line and said: "An old railway worker who lives near the track swears that a Trevithick locomotive ran on the line and that he has seen a photograph of it." The inference is that Mr Carr doubted the old man's statement, and one wonders if Mr Carr was imagining something like the Pen-y-darran locomotive built by Richard Trevithick, when of course the old man was referring to Richard's son, Francis, who was the Locomotive Superintendent at Crewe.

The Crewe Goods and the Goods Tanks which were Rams-bottom rebuilds of the tender engines, gave way to the more powerful Webb 4ft 8½in. 2–4–0 tanks or "Choppers". These arrived on the C&HP section in the mid-1890s, and one of the class, LNWR 2278, was destined to finish its working life on the

---

* *The Journal of the Stephenson Locomotive Society*, Vol. 27 (August 1951), pp. 205–210.
† Paper read before the Newcomen Society, Derby, 7 June 1934.

Sheep Pasture–Middleton stretch. "The Chopper", as it came to be called (being the last survivor of its class), bore four running numbers. Under London Midland & Scottish Railway ownership it became 6428 in 1928 (later prefixed by a 2), 26428 under British Railways in 1948, and finally 58092 in the BR general renumbering scheme. 58092 was withdrawn in March 1952, and its place was taken by the Kitson 0–4–0ST 47000. No. 2278 and another of the same class, 2244, were the inhabitants of the wooden locomotive shed at Middleton Top when that structure was completely destroyed by fire in 1906.

The year 1931 saw the arrival of the ex-North London Railway 0–6–0 side tanks, LMSR 7511 and 7521. These were very powerful machines, with a short wheelbase suited to the sharp curves of the line. Several engines of this class were allocated to Rowsley for the Cromford & High Peak Railway, subshedded at Cromford Wharf (one) and Middleton Top (two). Nos. 58850, 58856, and 58862 (BR numbers) all saw service in BR days. These engines performed their duties very well, and the sight and sound of one of them roaring up the Hopton Incline, showering the countryside with red-hot cinders from a plume of smoke and steam, is never forgotten.

One other class of engine which was represented on the High Peak was the Webb 0–4–2 square saddle tank. These engines came to be known as the Bissel Trucks, on account of the arrangement of the non-coupled axle. They were rather repulsive-looking locomotives with their square saddle tanks, which gave them a top-heavy appearance. The shunting duties at Cromford were the task of these engines, and Nos. 7859, 7861, and 7869 (LMS numbers) all spent some of their time in these placid surroundings.

North of Friden, which was used as an interchange station, traffic was handled by ex-Midland Railway 0–6–0 tender engines of class 3F, allocated to Buxton depot. These engines were also used for working the Hindlow to Ladmanlow section of the line. The section between Parsley Hay and Hindlow was used by larger forms of motive power such as the ex-LNWR 0–8–0, the 4F 0–6–0, and 8F 2–8–0 on freight turns, while the passenger traffic was handled by the parallel and taper boilered 2–6–4T of various classes built by the LMSR. The passenger service between Uttoxeter and Buxton which used this section was withdrawn on 30 October 1954.

British Railways standard engines did not appear on C&HP metals, and it is difficult to see where they could have been used except on the sections worked by the 0–6–0 3F locomotives. One wonders what might have happened if the scheme which was planned in the mid-19th century had been brought to fruition. This was to convert the whole line to main-line standards, inclined planes and all, and so avoid the expense of building a new line to link Manchester with the Midlands. It need hardly be said that the idea was soon shelved!

Before leaving the subject of motive power, mention must be made of the trials which were carried out with an engine designed by J.B. Fell on one of the inclines. These locomotives, designed for use on lines where severe gradients were encountered, had two sets of wheels placed horizontally between the frames, driven by separate cylinders, and gripping a raised central rail. E.L. Ahrons mentions these locomotives in his book *The British Steam Railway Locomotive, 1825–1925*, saying: "The first engine . . . was intended to test the system for application to the Mont Cenis Railway. It was tried on a track 800 yards long, of 3 ft 7⅜ in. gauge, laid on a gradient of 1 in 13½ on the High Peak Railway, Derbyshire."

Some controversy has arisen as to the actual site of the trials, which took place in two series between September 1863 and July 1865. In his book *Rambles on Railways*, published in 1868, Sir Cusack P. Roney wrote: "Early in 1863, Mr Fell instituted experiments on a length of 800 yards, laid to his plan, upon the Cromford & High Peak Railway near Whaley Bridge; the gauge was 3 ft 7½ in., 180 yards of the line was straight with a gradient of 1 in 13 (406 ft in 1 mile), 150 yards with a gradient of 1 in 12 (440 ft in 1 mile), with curves of 2½ chains radius". The Author has been given details by Mr W. Eyre of Whaley Bridge, of a diary kept by John Warren who lived in the same town. An entry dated 24 August 1863 is quoted as written: "the commenced altring the incline plain of the High Peak Realway at Whaley Bridge to work an Engin up the plain called the allpine Maid at Birkinhead on a new principel". This is interpreted as the name of the locomotive being the "Alpine" and it having been built in Birkinhead.

The Author is satisfied that the trials took place in Whaley Bridge although, at times, sites such as Hopton, and adjacent to the Bunsall incline have been put forward as possibilities.

An enthusiasts' special at Ladmanlow on the 25th April 1953 with No. 43618 in charge.
R.M. Casserley

Chapter 4
Working and Traffic

So far, mention has been made only of the methods of working employed on the inclined planes. The rest of the line where locomotive power was used is of interest by virtue of the variety of operating methods employed. The High Peak Junction to Cromford Goods section was worked on the "one engine in steam" principle, and as a siding. The isolated stretch from Sheep Pasture Top to Middleton Bottom was also "one engine in steam"; there was only one engine available anyway. From the top of Middleton Incline, the line was operated by train staff and ticket as far as Parsley Hay, in four sections, with dividing points at Hopton Top, Longcliffe Goods, and Friden. At Parsley Hay the line became a double track as far as Hindlow. This was controlled by the absolute block system with three block sections, Parsley Hay to Hurdlow, Hurdlow to Briggs Siding, and Briggs Siding to Hindlow. From Hindlow the line to Ladmanlow became single again, with the double track "main line" continuing towards Buxton. The single line was worked by train staff and ticket between Hindlow and Harpur Hill. The Harpur Hill to Old Harpur section, with its numerous sidings, was worked as a goods yard, and the remaining stretch from Old Harpur to Ladmanlow employed the same method as the opposite end of the line, one engine in steam. On the Cromford & High Peak line, therefore, five distinct methods of working were employed, including those used on the inclined planes.

Apart from the Parsley Hay to Hindlow sections, signals were virtually non-existent or, where they were to be found, were disused. Semaphore signals were in position at the top of the Sheep Pasture and Middleton Inclines. These were obviously of LNWR origin but towards the final days lost most of the glass from their spectacles. This loss was of no consequence, however, as there was no outdoor lighting anywhere on the line, and the timetable was arranged to confine train working to the hours of daylight. Another interesting signal, demolished in June 1950, was a two-armed double-facing signal, also of LNWR pattern, which controlled the junction with the Clay Cross Company's Grinn Branch at Ladmanlow (*see page 17*).

Since its construction, most of the traffic on the Cromford & High Peak Railway had been in local produce, mainly from the many limestone quarries. Before the Second World War, there was a daily (Sundays included) milk train to Buxton and Manchester which originated at Longcliffe, but this was discontinued during the war and was never reinstated.

WEEKDAYS — PARSLEY HAY AND MIDDLETON

DOWN

					J	J	J	J	J	J	J	
					8.10 am Empties from Buxton	7.55 am Empties from Buxton			1.35 pm from Hopton Quarry			
					74		74	75	74		75	
Mileage					FX	FO						
M	C				am	am	am	PM	am	PM	PM	
0	0	PARSLEY HAY	arr									
			dep		8 53	8 55						
2	26	Friden	arr		9 25	9 25						
			dep		9 40	9 40						
7	63	Longcliffe	arr					11 55				
			dep					12 25				
10	16	Hopton (Top)	arr					1 10				
			dep	8·15			12·0	1 23	2 0	1 45	2 40	
11	8	Hopton Quarry	arr	8 20						1 50		
			dep	8 30								
11	31	MIDDLETON (TOP)	arr	8 40			12 5	2 5	1 58		2 45	

UP

					J	J	J	J	J	J	J	J	
								To Hindlow		To Middleton	To Hindlow		
					74	75	74		74	74	75		
Mileage							SO			SX			
M	C				am	am	am	PM	PM	PM	PM	PM	
0	0	MIDDLETON (TOP)	dep		7 35	9 5	11 15		12 30		2 30		
0	23	Hopton Quarry	arr		7 45				12 40				
			dep		8 5								
1	15	Hopton (Top)	arr		8·10	9 15	11·20			1 35			
			dep			9 35				1 45	2 35		
1	77	Harboro' Sdgs	arr			9 40				1 50			
			dep			9 55							
3	48	Longcliffe	arr			10 5							
			dep			11 5							
9	5	Friden	arr			11 35							
			dep					12 30		1 55			
11	31	PARSLEY HAY	arr					12 45		2 13			

The working timetable of September 1956 to June 1957.
A scene on Hopton Incline in 1940 with the tank locomotive and brake van in full flight.

H.C. Casserley

The timetable which took effect in April 1874 was quite impos-
ing, with no fewer than 51 columns. There was one train daily
throughout the length of the line, in each direction. These trains
included the "fly" coach carrying passengers, to which reference
will be made later. The down train left High Peak Junction at
11.45 am and took five hours and twenty-five minutes to reach
Whaley Bridge at 5.10 pm. The up train had left Whaley Bridge at
9.20 am and took the same time, arriving at High Peak Junction at
2.45 pm. These trains crossed between Hopton and Middleton.
Several other trains were shown, with a total of nine departures
from High Peak Junction; eight terminated at Hopton, the other
ran through. There was also a 7.25 am from Sheep Pasture which
went through to Ladmanlow, arriving at 10.30 am; the corresponding working left Ladmanlow at 5.0 am and reached Sheep pasture
at 8.0 am. In addition to these, there were ten trips from Ladmanlow to Shallcross Yard and five from Harpur Hill to Ladmanlow; in
the up direction there were nine trips from Shallcross to Ladmanlow and five from Ladmanlow to Harpur Hill. there were also nine
departures from Hopton for the south, including the through train.
No mention was made anywhere of a Sunday service; it seems safe
to assume that there was none.

By 1891 the working timetable announced that on week-days
there would be one train in each direction between Cromford
(*bottom of*) and Whaley Bridge, and one train in each direction
between Cromford (*bottom of*) and Shallcross (*bottom of*). There was
also a schedule for a conditional train in each direction between
High Peak Junction and Whaley Bridge, to "run only by instructions from the Superintendent". A list of special instructions to be
observed when the specials were run was appended. It appears
that there were other trains running besides those mentioned, as in
the special instructions a train from Ladmanlow to Harpur Hill at
11.15 am which does not appear in the body of the table is told to
"stand clear of Ladmanlow, and show Staff No. 7 to Train No. 13
(the conditional train) and proceed after it at a steady speed".

By this time, the passenger service had been discontinued for
some years, having ceased in 1877 after a fatal accident which involved a passenger. The "fly" coach mentioned earlier was provided for the conveyance of travellers, who, however, had to
trudge up and down the various inclines. F.S. Williams, writing in
Our Iron Roads (1883 edition), gives a graphic description of a
journey over the Cromford and High Peak line, as described to him
by one of his friends.

The wheel-operated treadle that operated the warning gongs on Sheep Pasture Incline. *Author's Collection*

Two views of "hanging-on" (the term for coupling the wagons to the incline ropes), *left* at Middleton Top, and *right* at Sheep Pasture Bottom. *Author's Collection*

The "hanger-on" plaiting the chains round the incline rope (*top picture*). This chain was made with progressively smaller links which gave the chain a tapering effect and so tightened when under pressure. It was fastened off with leather thongs. Note additional chains around the buffers for added security (*bottom picture*).

LRGP, *Courtesy David and Charles*

The summit of Middleton Incline in May 1934 showing an early tender used throughout the railway for the conveyance of water. *H.C. Casserley*

Early LNWR McConnell locomotive, 4-wheeled tender used as a water carrier and numbered 11, standing at Sheep Pasture Bottom. The canal can be seen clearly behind the siding. *LRGP, Courtesy David and Charles*

"It was in August 1877", he (the friend) said, "and thinking I should like to see the country through which it passed, I went to Stonehouse, generally called 'Stonnis', just by the Black Rocks [this would be Steeplehouse], where the railway crosses the [Cromford to] Wirksworth road, and inquired of a man in the office for the train. 'Do you mean the "fly"?' was the reply. 'Yes.' But the official, not knowing whether the 'fly' had passed or not, went out to enquire, and brought back word that it had gone, but that if I followed it up the line, I might catch it at the siding, and if not, I should be sure to overtake it at 'Middleton Run'. I accordingly gave chase and at length caught sight of it being drawn up the incline by a rope and a stationary engine. A man at the bottom inquired if I wished to catch the 'fly', and added, 'I will stop it for you at the top', which he did by a signal. A quarter of a mile ahead I joined it. My fellow-travellers were then a young woman and a child, and the vehicle in which we sat was like an old omnibus. The guard stood in the middle and worked the brake through a hole in the floor. A locomotive now drew us three or four miles to the foot of another incline [Hopton] up which we were drawn by a rope. When reaching the summit the guard remarked, 'We may have to wait at the top.' 'How long?' I enquired. 'Oh! it may be five minutes,' he replied, 'or a few hours. It all depends upon when the engine comes to take us on. Yesterday,' he added, 'it did not come at all.' To while away the time I walked along the line, and my fellow-passengers went mushrooming. In about three hours an engine came from Whaley Bridge [?] to fetch us, and after the driver, fireman and guard had refreshed themselves at a little public house not far away, and had freely commented on their 'horse', they went back along the line, brought up the 'fly', and having refreshed themselves again, we started. At one part of the journey, a flock of sheep were quietly feeding or resting on the line. 'Just see them', said the guard as we approached, 'jump the walls'; and they did it like dogs. We reached Park Gates, about a mile from Buxton, at seven o'clock, after a journey of about twenty miles in six hours. Not long after my journey, a traveller on this line was killed, and the Company decided to close it against passenger traffic."

This account suggests that passengers were able to ride up the inclines, although others state that this was not so. Maybe the company's servants turned a blind eye if the passenger was prepared to take the risk of the rope breaking. It is also difficult to reconcile the time of arrival at Park Gates at 7 o'clock in the evening, and also the journey time of six hours to this point, although the carryings on at Hopton Top might account for that! At this rate of progress, Whaley Bridge would probably be reached at about 10 o'clock at night. These times do not agree with the timetable, although the estimated time from Steeplehouse at 1 o'clock can compare with the 12.35 pm departure advertised.

Since the passenger traffic ceased in 1877, there have been few occasions when passengers have travelled over the line. In 1932 an excursion from the firm of Mather and Platt penetrated as far as Friden, having travelled from Manchester via Buxton and Parsley

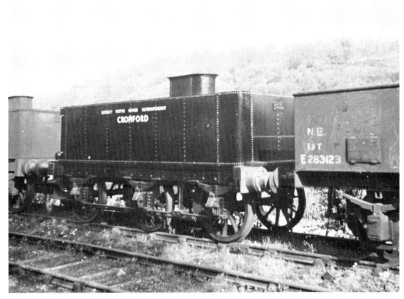

A further LNWR type of water carrying tender (marked District Motive Power Super-intendent, Cromford) seen here at Cromford Wharf. *Author's Collection*

Cromford Engine shed on the banks of the canal. *LGRP, Courtesy David and Charles*

Ex-North London Railway 0–6–0T, LMSR No. 27521 lying in the road below the embankment approaching Hopton Incline, after a derailment on 6 October 1937. Regrettably the driver, Mr Boden, was fatally injured in the mishap.

Derby Daily Telegraph

Retrieving 0–4–0ST No. 47000 from the cottage garden at Steeplehouse in July 1955, after becoming derailed when vandals altered the points. The fireman and driver luckily jumped clear.

Author's Collection

Hay. There were no station platforms at Friden; these existed only at Hindlow, Dowlow Halt, Hurdlow, and Parsley Hay.

In 1953, on two occasions, excursions covering the whole of the line from Cromford Wharf to Ladmanlow were organised by the Stephenson Locomotive Society and the Manchester Locomotive Society. The participants climbed the inclines at Sheep Pasture and Middleton on foot, being conveyed in open wagons between the two. From Middleton Top, a train of four open wagons and three brake vans was provided for the journey to Friden, the combined efforts of two North London tanks taking the train up Hopton Incline, at the top of which one of the engines was detached. From Friden to Ladmanlow a train of bogie coaches of the vestibule or "open" type took over, hauled by an ex-Midland Railway 3F 0-6-0.

The final timetables laid down timings between Middleton and Parsley Hay only, and shared a service in the up direction only. Only one train in each direction ran right through, and that was shown as Saturdays only. The remainder of the workings shown were between Middleton and Hopton, Middleton and Friden, and Friden and Parsley Hay.

To wind up this exploration of the line, another quotation seems appropriate; used in 1934 by D.S. Barrie and J.R. Hollick, to introduce their article on the C&HP Railway in the *Railway Magazine*, it was written a hundred and ten years ago by W. Adam in "The Gem of the Peak":

> "The High Peak Railway . . . is an interesting object; exhibiting a fine specimen of those intellectual energies given by a gracious God to man; and a striking proof of that passage that 'knowledge is power'; for who would have thought of a railway over such acclivities and apparently inaccessible tracts?"

Warning notice at Middleton Top on the C&HPR.
Author's Collection

Chapter 5
The Final Years

In the mid-1950s, the prospects on the line seemed to be bright, and traffic was increasing considerably. For example, Derbyshire Stone Firms who now controlled several quarries on the line estimated that they would despatch 140,000 tons of limestone in 1956. As the North London tanks were getting a bit long in the tooth, it was felt that they might not be able to cope, and alternatives were sought. The LMS Fowler dock tanks, and the War Department 0–6–0 saddle tanks were both proposed; 47164 was tried out on 17 February 1956 but, while it performed successfully and was considered suitable, as there were only ten engines in the class which had been built for dock work at places such as Fleetwood, the Operating Department decided that the dock tanks could not be spared. The War Department engines therefore found favour, but it was some time before they became established on the line. By early 1959, Nos. 68013 and 68030 were allocated to Middleton Top, while 68006 and 68034 were taking turns at Cromford Goods. No. 58850, now the last of the North London engines, returned to Middleton for a spell in May 1959, being used on a special train early in the month. By September, it was stored at Middleton, and the following year, at Rowsley. Withdrawn in September 1960, Derby works restored it as LNWR No. 2650 in October 1961, and it went to the Bluebell Railway early in 1962.

On the Sheep Pasture Top–Middleton Bottom section, No. 47007 replaced 47000 in 1958, remaining until November 1965 when No. 47000 returned. Steam was ousted on 26 August 1966, when a 204 hp diesel shunter, D2383 took over, following satisfactory tests. This locomotive remained on the section until Sheep Pasture incline was closed on 9 April 1967. Similar shunters had been in use at Cromford Goods from April 1965, being provided from Derby Motive Power Depot.

On the upper section between Middleton and Friden, a 350 hp diesel-electric shunter was tried out in late August 1966, but presumably was found to be wanting as the J94 engines continued to monopolise the section.

The winding engine at Sheep Pasture incline was beginning to feel its age in 1957 and it became obvious that very extensive repairs and renewals would be needed. There was very considerable traffic on the incline, most of it limestone from Hopton Wood Stone Firms quarry on the Killers branch. It was decided that new electric winding gear was justified and this was brought into operation early in 1965. The whole installation was completely new, and consisted of a pair of pulleys of similar size to the original ones, but fabricated in steel. The lower pulley was driven by a hundred horse power electric motor through a fluid coupling, a reduction gear box and a final pair of reduction gears. There was also a large brake drum on the lower pulley shaft. The run of the ropes was as on the earlier winding engines, each pulley having two grooves to take the ropes. With the new equipment, an unbalanced load of 60 tons downwards or 10 tons upwards could be handled on the incline.

At the time the new equipment was installed, the ex-LNWR signal which stood at the top of the incline and which might have at one time controlled descending runs, was replaced by a modern upper quadrant semaphore. The purpose of this substitution was obscure, as the signal, whenever the author was watching operations was always "ON" and appeared to be purely decorative!

Before leaving Sheep Pasture, mention must be made of a runaway which occurred on 28 September 1965. Two wagons ran into the catch pit, the reason given being a combination of brake failure and a greasy rope.

The Middleton engine continued to work right up until the incline was closed on 12 August 1963. A couple of years earlier, new segments were fitted into the winding pulleys of the engine. The Middleton Run became redundant with the decline of traffic on the Middleton–Friden section, which took place in the early sixties; this was the result of increasing road competition and also the closure of some of the quarries on the section. To illustrate the rapid changes of fortune which can occur, the case of the Magnesium-Elektron factory at the bottom of Hopton can be cited. Here was a large factory which was built in the early 'sixties to produce magnesium from dolomite, and which was expected to have a considerable rail traffic to it. A siding was provided, with direct discharge to conveyor belts to feed the imported reducing agent into the plant. Opened in March 1963, by June 1966 the factory had closed as, due to a slump in the market for magnesium, it had become uneconomic.

Going back to Middleton, the rails were lifted in November 1964. The wire ropes were cut off outside the engine house, being left in position round the pulleys. The engine could, however, still be run light, out of mesh with the pulleys. This was necessary to pump water into the tank for locomotive purposes, and to provide feedwater for the stationary engine and its condenser. In 1966 at Christmas vandals smashed most of the brass boiler fittings, making the engine incapable of use. They were caught, but the damage

BRITISH RAILWAYS
L.M.R.

E.R.O. 46495

GREEN
UP. TRAIN STAFF TICKET

CROMFORD AND HIGH PEAK LINE

TRAIN No..........................

TO THE DRIVER

5925

You are authorised, after seeing the Train Staff for the
Section, to proceed from

MIDDLETON TOP TO HOPTON TOP

and the Train Staff will follow

Signature of

Date............................ *Person In charge*............................

This Ticket must be given by the Driver, immediately on arrival,
to the person in charge of the Staff Working at the place to which
he is authorised to proceed, to be cancelled and forwarded to the
Chief Operating Superintendent.

B.R. 25559/1

BRITISH RAILWAYS

NOT TRANSFERABLE

FORM OF PERMIT

ELEVEN PEOPLE

The Bearer M⁅ .....⁆ .. Rummel .... ★and ~~ONE PERSON~~
travelling in attendance is are authorised on the payment of the appropriate fare(s)
to travel in the van with the Guard or in another vehicle not usually provided for the
accommodation of passengers.

† { By ~~any British Railways~~ echos Train
{ between MIDDLETON TOP .... Station and FRIDEN· ....Station
subject to prior notice being given of each intended journey to the Station Master at
the starting point ★(and to accommodation being available in non-passenger
carrying vehicle by the selected service for the conveyance of the invalid vehicle).

Valid from............ 21ˢᵗ APRIL 1967 to............ ONLY............ 19......

Signature of authorised Officer ....

.... Station .... Region

★Delete if not required.

Date............ 14/4/1967

† Delete words not applicable.

Permit for party to travel on last service train, *see page 95.*

The last service train descending Hopton Incline on 21 April 1967 with No. 68012 hauling a brake van special and inscribed appropriately "Journey's End".

Derby Evening Telegraph

Ticket for party on last service train, *see page 95.*

British Railways Board (M)

ISSUED AT..

AI 071344

FROM...*MIDDLETON TOP*................ ( )

TO ....*FRIDEN*.................... ( )

○ **UTWARD JOURNEY**

Route ....

For alternative routes enquire at Booking Office.   *BR RESEARCH DEPT DERBY PART-Y*

DESCRIPTION		PASSENGERS NO. (in words)	FARE	AMOUNT £ s. d.			
ORDINARY FULL FARE	Adults						CLASS *SECOND*
	Children ...						
FORCES DUTY	Officers ...		—	—	—	—	Valid — *ONE*
	O/Ranks ...		—	—	—	—	Outward. ...†days/months
GROUP TRAVEL	Adults						*ONE* Return.......†days/months
	Children under 14 ...						Commencing Date
	Young persons under 18 ...						*21ˢᵗ April* 19.*67*
Other Descriptions *BRAKE VAN*	Adults	*TWELVE*	*5/-*	*3*	*0*	*0*	(Month in words)
	Children ...						Warrant No. *155/214/1321*

* To be completed (in words) at time of issue   † Delete as necessary

NOT TRANSFERABLE

Amount Paid *3 0 0*

Issued subject to The Conditions and Regulations in the Board's Publications and Notices.   BR 4404/2

Two views of a train of "open wagons" enthusiast special on 25 April 1953, with No. 47000 in charge, seen here at Sheep Pasture Top. *H.C. Casserley*

was done. As the original boilers were worn out, an ex-locomotive boiler had been used to supply steam. This was cut up on site in March 1967, while the earlier boilers remain. After this, water was brought in the mobile tanks from Buxton, and pumped up into the tank with a small petrol-driven pump.

While on the subject of the inclines, the old Bunsall Incline came into use for a period between 1962 and 1967, albeit by the motor lorry. This was in connection with the construction of a dam across the Goyt Valley to provide a second reservoir, and the old pack-horse road and the Bunsall Incline were surfaced to give road access for bringing in plant and materials from the Buxton–Whaley Bridge Road.

As we have seen, the bright prospects had begun to dim in the 'sixties as the motor lorry took over the staple traffic on the line, particularly on the top section. From 1961, one engine was allocated to Middleton, and towards the end of the service, only ran a train on Mondays, Wednesdays and Fridays. Even this scanty service was not always necessary and the engine would go to Parsley Hay and back to fetch tanks of water for later journeys, or so that the train crew could collect their wages. In early 1967, the water position at Middleton had become so desperate, following a particular mild and dry winter, that on one occasion the engine crew had prepared their engine and were praying that Buxton had sent a tank of water to Parsley Hay, as, if not, they reckoned they would have to wait for rain to fill up the reservoir at Middleton before they would have enough water for another preparation and journey! Buxton had sent a tank so the situation was saved.

Mention of one mild winter leads to the one of 1962–63 when very severe weather occurred. During this winter, the locomotive shed at Sheep Pasture Top was blown down, while the one at Middleton lost its roof. On 21 January 1963, all roads to the village of Hartington were completely blocked by snow and provisions had to be sent from Ashbourne and Buxton by rail. Snow ploughs were used to keep the line clear and on one occasion a plough train became stuck and was retrieved by digging out several hours later.

The C & HP line had, since World War II, become a firm favourite with railway enthusiasts and excursions over the line had become quite a feature. Some of these have been referred to in earlier chapters, and mention has already been made of the special which was run on 3 May 1959, when the last of the North London tanks was used. This excursion started from Northampton and was advertised as "the last opportunity for railway enthusiasts to travel on this historic line". Why such terms were used is not clear as there was no threat of closure at that time.

A rail tour was organised jointly by the Stephenson and Manchester Locomotive Societies on 30 September 1961, and the same two bodies ran a trip over the line from north to south on 4 March 1967.

The line also had what might be termed "internal" visits from parties of BR staff. For example a District Engineers Conference at Buxton in February 1957 took the opportunity to visit the line, and had an excellent hand-out prepared. The author has been fortunate enough to see a copy, which has settled the vexed question of the superelevation on Gotham curve. This is stated to have been 10⅛ inches up until 1945, after which date it was altered to ⅝ inch. Another interesting fact was that the length of line between 19½ and 19 mileposts, approaching Hopton Incline is completely unrestricted as to speed, a distinction which can be claimed by few lengths of main line, which normally have some limit imposed.

The Line Manager's Office staff at Derby went over the line on 7 April 1962, and their visit was written up in the London Midland magazine the following July.

In March and April, 1967, some of the service trains were used by small groups of people, with the blessing of the BR Public Relations Department in Manchester, to pay a final visit to the railway. The author was able to organise such a tour on the last day of service, 21 April 1967, with a group of friends. There was one particular feature of the outing which is worth recounting.

The train crew working from Middleton had all been declared redundant, and this was to be their last job. As Manchester had fixed the tour, it was necessary to bring the brake van back to Middleton, after which the engine was to go to Buxton to be ready to work the final excursion on the line, nine days later, on 30 April. So when the train reached Parsley Hay, it was met by a second engine crew who were coming to take the engine back to Buxton. There was also a second driver who, because four sets of men would be needed for the two engines being employed on 30 April, had come out to "learn the road". This must surely be unique in railway history for a driver to be road-learning on the last day of regular service!

And so to Sunday 30 April 1967. A heavy programme was planned with three round trips between Middleton and Parsley Hay, the first for the Birmingham Area of the SLS, and the others in conjunction with an excursion using Flying Scotsman from Kings Cross to Chesterfield and visiting the C&HPR and the Crich Tramway Museum by motor coach.

The start of the first run was delayed by late arrival at Middleton of the train from Buxton, consisting of two J94 engines, Nos. 68006 and 68012, and six brake vans. Further delay occurred as the train stalled on Hopton Incline, necessitating reversal to the bottom, dividing and taking the vans up in two lots of three. All this activity delighted the throngs of enthusiasts at the line side, whose cars jammed the narrow roads round Middleton and Hopton. There was also a much longer stop for water than was allowed in the timings.

Only four brake vans were brought back from Parsley Hay in the hope that the second assault on Hopton would be successful. However, it was not to be. The run up from Hopton tunnel was too vigorous so that the engines were "winded" and they stalled again on the 1 in 20. Much to the horror of railwaymen in the watching crowd, the brakes were screwed down hard on the rear two vans and they were left on the incline while the engines took the front pair up. They came back for the second pair and were coupled on without incident, and the train was made up again at the top. To try to offset the further delay this trip ran only to Friden.

The third run started very late, and was run only to Longcliffe as the participants had to get to Chesterfield for their return to London. The relief engine crews had now taken over and with the ex-regular Middleton driver on one engine and his fireman riding with the other driver, a successful climb of Hopton was made, the summit being breasted at a slow walking pace, despite a brief slip by one engine lower down.

A similar ascent was made as pale sunlight cast long shadows and the empty (?) stock was taken away, terminating in a fitting manner a history extending over 142 years. Trains to collect odd wagons and water tanks ran during the first week in May leaving the line derelict and weed-grown. The Friden to Parsley Hay section remained open until September 1967 after which time the Cromford and High Peak Railway joined the long list of lines whose usefulness has ended, but which will be remembered for many years to come.

Chapter 6
After Closure

By the time of closure, the track had already been lifted between High Peak Junction and Middleton Top, and it was not long before dismantling began from Middleton to Parsley Hay and on to Dowlow. There was a proposal put forward for preservation from Middleton Top to Longcliffe and Parsley Hay, with the prospectus talking of steam hauled trains carrying tourists over the line. Basic items like provision of water, which was being brought from Buxton in rail tanks at the time of closure, and the problems of track maintenance over the inhospitable moorland were carefully ignored. Needless to say, the promoters of the scheme found little enthusiasm was shown and no more was heard of it.

Over the next few years, the Derbyshire County Council and the Peak District National Park Board acquired the track bed between Cromford Wharf and Hurdlow, and also the formation of the former Ashbourne to Buxton line south of Parsley Hay to Ashbourne, and converted these into the High Peak Trail and the Tissington Trail respectively, over which it is possible to walk, cycle or ride on horseback. Car parking facilities have been provided at certain places, also picnic areas, and toilets and cycle hire points are included at some locations. For the benefit of the present-day visitor, it is proposed to work through the line from south to north as was done in Chapter 2 and give details of access and features of note. Map references are given, and are based on the Ordnance Survey Pathfinder Series 1:25000 sheets, the sheet numbers also being quoted. Five sheets cover the whole line from Cromford Wharf to Whaley Bridge.

Cromford Wharf becomes the starting point, as the stretch down to the site of High Peak Junction is not included in the Trail. The map reference for the Wharf on sheet SK25/35 is 313559. There is no car park there, access being for walkers, cyclists and horse riders. There is a picnic area adjacent to the workshops, which are named "High Peak Junction Workshops" although strictly the signal box and junction of that name were over a mile away. The workshops are being renovated (1984) and the intention is to reproduce a scene shown in an early photograph of the interior. Adjacent to the canal, which has been cleared of weeds and made navigable to Cromford Meadows by the Cromford Canal Society, is the Transit Shed which has been converted for use as a countryside pursuits centre for groups of up to 28 persons in self catering accommodation, and is administered by the Derbyshire County Council. The Canal Society operate a horse drawn "water bus"

Wirksworth Incline showing the overgrown formation with Wirksworth Station visible beyond the bridge in the centre of the photograph.   *LGRP, Courtesy David and Charles*

Middleton Bottom Cutting situated at the top of the incline to Wirksworth.
LGRP, Courtesy David and Charles

between the Wharf and the end of the Canal at the Meadows, and they have also restored the Leawood Pumping Engine, a huge single cylinder beam engine which pumps water from the River Derwent to maintain the level in the canal. This engine is steamed occasionally, usually at Bank Holidays, a charge being made for entry to the engine house to help defray expenses.

If we now return to the Workshops, and walk with them on our right, we are at the bottom of Sheep Pasture Incline. The horizontal wheel round which the winding rope passed has had the pit covers removed, and it is possible to see how the wheel could be moved to take up slack in the rope. The water tanks which used to store the water sent out in the rail tanks are on the left, while ahead as we start up the incline, is the bridge carrying the A6 road from Derby to Matlock. This is now much narrower than when the railway was operating as the bridge was strengthened in 1981–2. Beyond the bridge is the catch pit described in Chapter 2, into which it is possible to descend, to find the remains of the last run-away, in a very sorry state, with heavily rusted iron work and crumbling rotting timbers. It is without means of identification, other than that it was a five-plank wooden wagon, and is believed to have belonged to ICI.

Continuing up the incline, the site of the winding engine house is reached, and then it is easy walking on the level to Black Rocks (map reference 290557). At this point there is a car park, picnic site and toilets in a small purpose built structure, which also serves refreshments in the summer months. A map is displayed outside the building giving details of walks in the vicinity.

Continuing along the Trail, we reach the Middleton Incline, having passed on our way across the bridge over the Cromford to Wirksworth road and seen on the right where the branch to Hoptonwood Stone Firms Middleton quarry left the line. At Middleton Bottom, to the left, it is possible to see where the incline from Wirksworth would have been sited.

Ascending the Middleton Incline, we cross three bridges, the second being the original crossing the Middleton to Brassington road and now disused, and the third larger span being a new structure built when the road was diverted to meet the needs of traffic for reservoir construction at Carsington. Reaching Middleton Top, dominated by the winding house chimney, we find a large car park, picnic area, and a visitor centre with a shop, cycle hire point and toilets, as well as the winding engine house. The map reference is 276552. The winding engine has been restored and is run on air pressure on the first Saturday in each month, from 2 pm to 4 pm, Easter to the end of September. Plans are afoot (1985) to obtain a boiler to enable the engine to be run under steam at some time in the future.

The Trail continues, passing through Hopton Tunnel and across the embankment leading to Hopton Incline. At the road bridge, the formation of the siding down into Hopton Quarry can be seen on the right, and beyond the bridge on the same side is the dolomite processing factory. At Hopton Top (map reference 253546), Hopton Cottage has been renovated (and now has piped water!) and is used to provide basic accommodation for ramblers and hikers, arrangements for booking being similar to those for the Cromford Transit Shed. There is access to the Trail nearby for walkers and cyclists, but no car park.

Moving on with Harborough Rocks a significant feature on the right, the route continues to Longcliffe (map reference 226557). As at Hopton Top, no provision is made for car parking, access being just for walkers and cyclists. The site has been landscaped, with ample areas of grass, but the table and bench picnic site units are not provided here.

The next access point at Minninglow takes us on to Sheet SK05/15, map reference 194581. Here there is a car park and picnic area, and waymarked paths to provide a choice of three circular walks, start and finish at the car park, being detailed on leaflets available from a weatherproof dispenser. A longer scenic tour of 25 miles is also given, intended for motorists.

Newhaven Crossing (map reference 181598) is on the A5012 road and is about halfway to Friden, access at the crossing being limited to walkers and cyclists, no car park. At Friden, Sheet SK06/16, map reference 172607, provision is the same as at Minninglow, car park, picnic site and leaflets to describe walks from this point in the surrounding area.

Following the trail onwards past the Silica Firebrick Works, the pathway passes through Newhaven Road Tunnel with its plaques on the stone facing at either end, and a short distance further on reaches Parsley Hay (map reference 146637) with the Tissington Trail joining our route from the left as we approach the site of the station. In the old yard, there is a car park, picnic area, and amenity block with toilets and a cycle hire point. A map of the surrounding area, giving prominence to the Trails, is displayed outside.

Leaving Parsley Hay, the High Peak Trail follows a general north-westerly direction to Sparklow (map reference 128659). It is possible to pick out the old formation before the easing of the sharp curves about halfway along this section, near to Cotesfield Farm.

Restored cottages at Hopton Top.
Author's Collection

Middleton Incline showing new and old bridges. *Author's Collection*

Signal post, workshops etc., at Cromford Wharf. *Author's Collection*

Monument at Bunsall Bottom recording use of inclines in the construction of the water reservoirs. *Author's Collection*

At Sparklow, which is named Hurdlow (!), there is a car park and picnic area. Just beyond the road over-bridge, the line of the original Hurdlow Incline can be seen quite clearly climbing the hill-side to the left, while the Trail follows the deviation made to eliminate the stationary engine working. It is possible to continue for about 1½ miles beyond Hurdlow (or Sparklow) to the north end of the High Peak Trail (map reference 111673). A right turn up the track takes us up to the A515 road which is 400 yards away, and on which there is a lay-by 100 yards to the right. Dowlow Lime Works is still rail-connected and prevents access northwards.

It is now necessary to move to Sheet SK07/17, to see where access can be gained to the old track formation in Harpur Hill, turning left into Haslin Road (a cul-de-sac) when approaching from the south (map reference 067704). The original and later formations are clearly visible, the lower line having come from Hindlow, while the upper, older, track ended its days as a siding serving Hillhead Quarry. The junction at Harpur Hill is clearly seen, and it is possible to follow the well-trodden path as far as map reference 058707, on the road giving access to Harpur Hill Industrial Estate.

Beyond this point, access is forbidden although it is possible to trace where the line ran on its way to Ladmanlow (map reference 041767). The site of Ladmanlow Yard, now the private garden of the level crossing cottage on the A53 road, is well defined. The bridge abutment at the north end of the yard remains alongside the A54 Buxton–Macclesfield road and from here the bridge which carried Old Macclesfield Road is clearly seen, with the wagon-turning triangle nearer to the observer, while beyond the bridge, the line can be seen receding towards Burbage Tunnel.

The next access point is beyond the tunnel at Bunsall Top (map reference 024752). This is reached by a narrow road off the A5002 Buxton–Whaley Bridge road on the left signposted "Goyt Valley" (map reference 032752); there is a car park adjacent to a small reservoir. From here, one can turn left and walk to the north portal of Burbage Tunnel, noting on the way where a small valley has been crossed by two embankments, with presumably the larger being built to ease the sharp curve of the one nearer the top of the valley.

Alternatively, if we turn right, we reach the Bunsall Inclines. As mentioned in Chapter 5, these are now a paved roadway, and vehicular access is possible to the bottom, and then across the dam to car parking and picnic areas. Before crossing the dam, there is a toilet block alongside the road (closed in winter) and almost op-posite this is a plaque recording the use of the old railway to con-struct the dam, erected by the Stephenson Locomotive Society, and incorporating one of the original stone sleepers. From a point a few yards away, a footpath makes it possible to walk along the former trackbed alongside the Lower Goyt reservoir, to the lower dam (map reference 015728). This point can also be reached by car from the A5002 by a roadway marked North West Water, Eastern Region, Fernilee Treatment Works (map reference 017783). There is no access northwards beyond the lower dam.

At map reference 016788, the A5002 is carried on filling over the old trackbed, which can be seen on both sides of the road here-abouts, although access is difficult and probably pointless.

The remaining accesses are all at Whaley Bridge. As the town is approached, a right turn into New Road, just before a traffic light controlled crossroads leads to a complex of flats called Cromford Court. These are in fact built in Shallcross Yard, and a footpath towards the town leads to the yard throat, and a bridge under the A6 road. The map sheet is now SK08/18 and the reference 012805. Alongside the path is a commemorative monument in the form of a stone-built wheel and an original fish-belly rail, with the Cromford and High Peak Railway arms in the hub. In Whaley Bridge, beyond the bridge referred to above, the line has been made into a "Linear Park". It is not possible to follow right from here to the top of Whaley Bridge Incline as a contractor's yard blocks the way, neces-sitating a detour. Regaining the track bed, we walk down the incline, noting the area on the right at the top where the horse capstan once stood. At the bottom, the pathway crosses a bridge over the River Goyt and gives access to the wharves alongside the Peak Forest Canal, now busy with leisure craft. The map reference is 012817 and there is a car park nearby.

So our journey over the former Cromford and High Peak Rail-way is completed, it still being possible to walk or cycle over about two thirds of the original route, virtually all of which can be traced out on the maps.

Brief details of the Tissington Trail which follows the LNWR line north from Ashbourne to Parsley Hay are as follows.

Access can be gained at Mapleton Lane, Ashbourne (map refer-ence 175469), Thorpe (map reference 166503), Tissington (map reference 178521), Alsop-en-le-Dale (map reference 156549), Hart-ington (map reference 150611) and Parsley Hay (map reference 146637). The first four are on map SK05/15, while the other two are on SK06/16. Cycle hire can be arranged at Mapleton Lane and Parsley Hay, there are car parks and picnic sites at all six places, and toilets are provided at Tissington and Parsley Hay.

Bibliography

The following sources have been consulted in the preparation of this book:

J. Jessop, 'High Peak Steam Railway, Second Report' (Derby 1824).

J. Priestley, 'Historical Account of the Navigable Rivers, Canals, and Railways of Great Britain' (1831).

E. Bradbury, 'In the Derbyshire Highlands' (1881).

F.S. Williams, 'Our Iron Roads' (1883 ed.).

H.G. Lewin, 'Early British Railways, 1801–1844' (1925).

E.L. Ahrons, 'The British Steam Railway Locomotive, 1825–1925' (1927).

C.F. Dendy Marshall, 'A History of British Railways Down to the Year 1830' (1938).

H.F.F. Livesey, 'The Locomotives of the L.N.W.R.' (1948).

L.T.C. Rolt and P.B. Whitehouse, 'Lines of Character' (1952).

Journal of the Derbyshire Archaeological and Natural History Society:
E.C. Eagle, 'Abstracts of Acts relating to the Cromford & High Peak Railway', 8 (1934), 40; D.P. Carr, 'Sidelights on the Cromford & High Peak Railway', 8 (1934), 45.

The Railway Gazette:
'Incline Working on the L.M.S.R.', 68 (1938), 599.

The Railway Magazine:
D.S. Barrie and J.R. Hollick, 'The Cromford & High Peak Railway', 75 (1934), 353; 76 (1935), 142, 302; 77 (1935), 61 (by W. Walker), 301, (by K. Brown); 'The High Peak Railway in Wartime', 90 (1944), 152.

Journal of the Stephenson Locomotive Society:
C. & H.P.R. Locomotives, 27 (1951), 205 (by G.J. Aston), 292 (by D. Cole), 294 (by P.C. Dewhurst), 295 (by E. Craven); 28 (1952), 69, 149 (by S.H.P. Higgins); 31 (1955), 116 (by E. Craven), 189, 206 (by G. Taylor and C.R. Clinker).

Transactions of the Newcomen Society:
B. Baxter, 'Early Railways in Derbyshire' 26 (1949), 185*Railway Magazine*, January 1961. 'Fells Experimental Railway in Derbyshire'. W.H. Hoult.

Railway World, March 1967.

The Locomotive Magazine, The Engineer, and *Engineering*.

'A Pictorial Guide to the High Peak and Tissington Railways'. Peak Park Planning Board/Derbyshire County Council.